Violence Against Women in Northeast India

Violence Against Women in Northeast India

with special reference to Assam, Manipur and Tripura

Edited by

H. Sudhir

Jubita Hajarimayum

AKANSHA PUBLISHING HOUSE

NEW DELHI-110 002(INDIA)

AKANSHA PUBLISHING HOUSE
4649/21B, Ansari Road
Darya Ganj, New Delhi-2
Phone : 23263193, 9811582579
Email : ektabooks@yahoo.com

Violence Against Women in Northeast India

First Published, 2005
ISBN : 81-87606-99-1

PRINTED IN INDIA

Published by M.P. Misra for Akansha Publishing House, New Delhi-110059 and Printed at Tarun Offset Press, Delhi.

Foreword

This present volume *Violence Against Women in Northeast India* (with special reference to Assam, Manipur and Tripura), is a product of a three-day regional seminar under the same name, a first-of-its-kind of venture in India's Northeast, organized by the Erema Gender Empowerment and Resource Centre, Manipur under the sponsorship of the Indian Council of Social Science Research (ICSSR), New Delhi at Imphal, Manipur during 21-23 August, 2003. The seminar was conceptualized on collaborative partnership for government, non-government, institutions of civil society, social researchers and activists representing the three sister states of this region viz., Assam, Manipur and Tripura as a part of our odyssey to have a deeper understanding of this serious problem, to develop integrated strategies, to respond effectively to it and to enhance prevention intervention in this vulnerable social target group–Women. Stemming from the conviction that the progress of the society in the northeast today also has its practical meaning in understanding the issue, the seminar represents one forward step in the process of assembling a human resource of the region committed to ushering in a culture of progress. The uniqueness of the seminar is in its dedication in expediting to bridge the wide gulf between the research findings and practices.

Though this region has shown a growing instance of violence against women in varying degrees, this serious issue has to remain for long unfocused. Sensing urgency to sensitize this crucial issue and a need for a creative thought that can facilitate to a better understanding of this violent issue, the perspective of the seminar was crucially designed to create a platform to explore and discourse upon the extent, dynamics and problem of violence against women in the region; examine the overall impact at varying degrees; impact of advocacy and public awareness campaign; social attitude; evaluate national and state responses; and develop viable intervention strategies for effective implementations. It is indeed a matter of joy that this initiative bore fruit in the form of bringing forth this present anthology of revised seminar papers as a piecemeal contribution to the larger phenomenon of the issue of violence against women. I am hopeful that this volume will be invaluable for social researchers, academicians, policy makers, administrators, practitioners and activists in India and abroad.

March 8, 2005
Imphal

Jubita Hajarimayum
Secretary
Ereima Gender Empowerment and Resource Centre

Preface

One area of primacy as a parcel of the broader analysis of the gender issue is the serious concern of violence against women in the northeast region of India. As part of its objective to provide a forum for cordial relationship and interaction among the people from varied professional expertises in the search for a creative understanding of the current scene of violence against women in the northeast, the Ereima Gender Empowerment and Resource Centre (EGERC), sensing it a need of the hours, initiated a three day regional seminar on Violence against women in Northeast India (with special reference to Assam, Manipur and Tripura), under the auspices of the Indian Council of Social Science Research ICSSR), New Delhi during 21-23 August 2003 at Imphal, Manipur

The seminar was structured aiming at shedding light on the state of violence against women in this part of India. Broadly, the seminar aims to develop enabling collaborative platform for different professional backgrounds to respond effectively to the problem of violence against women in the region. Specially the seminar aimed to sensitize the problem of violence against women in the region, create a platform to explore the issue by accessing information from different resource persons, organizations and individuals regarding the extent, dynamics and problem of the gender based violence, monitor and evaluate the impact of advocacy and problem awareness, disseminate the experiences, wisdom and findings of various organizations, institutions and individuals in the region to challenge the issue successfully.

Despite the higher social role and status of women in this region against her counterparts in other parts of India, women here face a variety of violences in varied forms due to a number of contributing factors in different contextual settings, which are explored herein by the paper contributors.

The present volume is a compilation of selected papers after revision and modification in the light of the discourse during seminar. The successful organization of the seminar and its translation into this crystallized current shape owe to many capacities for their support and co-operation in various forms. We acknowledge with gratitude to the Indian Council of Social Science Research (ICSSR), New Delhi for the financial assistance through which the initiative could be materialized successfully.

We are grateful to all the resource persons for the sacrifices made to come all the ways to present the papers personally and handing over their revised papers for publication. We are grateful to the support staff at the center for their unrelenting co-operation in the successful organization of the seminar and towards translating it into this present shape of the volume. Mention may be made of Rk Joyshree, Bhavina Sharma, Lakhikanta, Bimol, Sushil and Suresh. We thank Mr. M.P.Misra of Akansha Publising House, New Delhi for his keen interest and warm co-operation in publishing the volume.

The publication of this volume has been a little delayed because of the time given to the authors to modify and revise their papers and tedious editorial challenge.

A painstaking editorial task has been carried out yet it can be once more shared in the meantime that all the views expressed in the articles are of the authors entirely and they do not reflect the ideas of the editors or the institute.

H. Sudhir
Jubita Hajarimayum

Content

Content

List of Tables

List of Diagrams

Contributors

Dr. Vasudha Gupta is Deputy Secretary, Department of Women and Child, Government of India.

Dr. Archana Sharma is Director, Women's Studies Research Centre, Gauhati University, Guwahati, Assam.

Indranoshee Das is Junior Research Fellow, Women's Studies Research Centre, Guwahati University, Guwahati, Assam.

Dr. Dilip K. Medhi is Reader in Anthropology, Guwahati University, Guwahati, Assam.

Esther Chinnu is coordinator with the NorthEast Network (NEN), Manipur.

Dr. Salam Irene is Reader in History, Manipur University, Imphal, Manipur.

Dr. N. Vijaylakshmi Brara is sociologist working on gender issues.

Minakshi Sen Bandyopadhyay is a Member-Secretary, Tripura State Commission for Women, Agartala, Tripura.

Paramita Saha is Lecturer, Depaprtment of Economics, Tripura University, Agartala, Tripura.

1

Note on Violence Against Women

—Vasudha Gupta

Introduction

The term 'violence against women' means any act of gender-based violence that results in, or is likely to result in, physical, sexual or psychological harm or suffering to women, including threats of such acts, coercion or arbitrary deprivation of liberty, whether occurring in public or private life. Accordingly, violence against women encompasses, but is not limited, to the following:

- Physical, sexual and psychological violence occurring in the family, including battering, sexual abuse of female children in the household, dowry-related violence, female genital mutilation and other traditional practices harmful to women, non-spousal violence and violence related to exploitation;
- Physical, sexual and psychological violence occurring within the community, including rape, sexual abuse, sexual harassment and intimidation at work, in educational institutions and elsewhere, trafficking in women and forced prostitution;

In addition to the above, there could be acts of violence against women, which include forced sterilization and forced abortion, coercive/forced use of contraceptives, female infanticide and pre-natal sex selection.

Acts or threats of violence, whether occurring within the home or in the community, instill fear and insecurity in women's lives and are obstacles to the achievement of equality and for development and peace. The fear of violence, including harassment, is a permanent constraint on the mobility of women and limits their access to resources and basic activities.

The strategic objectives of the Beijing Platform for Action suggest adoption of a 'holistic and multi-disciplinary approach to the challenging tasks of promoting families, communities and state that are free of violence against women'. There has been extensive recognition by Government and society of the growing trends in cases of violence against women.

There are altogether international efforts for addressing violence against women and the main instruments are: UN Convention on the Elimination of all Forms of Discrimination Against Women (CEDAW), World Conference on Human Rights - Vienna, UN International Conference on Population and Development - Cairo and UN Fourth World Conference on Women - Beijing, 1995.

Violence against women - Situation in India

Women in India are vulnerable to various forms of violence based on gender due to unequal relationship between men and women.

- Because a woman is considered a weaker sex both in terms of physical strength and in having a say in the socio-cultural set up. They are subjected to physical violence like rape, female infanticide, and sex-related crimes. This reason is the understanding of society of female sexuality and its role in social hierarchy.
- Because of her relationship *vis-à-vis* man, a woman is vulnerable to domestic violence, dowry murder etc. This reason relates to society's concept of a woman as the

property and dependent on a male protector, father, husband, son etc.

- Because of the social group to which she belongs, a woman, in times of war, riots or ethnic, caste or class violence, may be raped and brutalized as a means of humiliating the community to which she belongs. This also relates to male perception of female sexuality and woman as the property of man.

The National Crimes Records Bureau (NCRB) under the Ministry of Home Affairs, Government of India has been collecting and recording data on gender based violence. The statistical data compiled by the Bureau on crimes against women during the years from 1990-2001 (Annexure A) show that there is an increasing trend in violent acts committed. The increase may, to an extent, reflect the effect of spread of literacy, awareness generated among women to their rights and legal protection that have been strengthened in the last two decades and the willingness of women to come out and seek help be it violence by third party or from within a family. On the other hand, judicial activism, NGO intervention, and law enforcement agencies' willingness to take cognizance of crime against women have together contributed to an increased reporting of cases. Women now approach police or courts more freely for remedy.

Legislative Measures - Legal Rights of Women

Women could also be victims of forced violence or crime commonly recognized such as 'Murder', 'Robbery', 'Cheating' etc. The crimes, which are directed specifically against women, are characterized as 'Crimes Against Women'. These are broadly classified under two categories: -

(1) The crimes identified under the Indian Penal Code (IPC)

(i) Rape (Section 376 IPC).

(ii) Kidnapping & abduction for different purposes (Section 363 - 373 IPC).

(iii) Homicide for Dowry, Dowry Deaths or their attempts (Section 302/304-B of IPC).

(iv) Torture, both mental and physical (Section 498-A of IPC).

(v) Molestation (Section 354 of IPC).

(vi) Sexual harassment (Section 509 of IPC) (referred to in the past as Eve-teasing)

(vii) Importation of girls (upto 21 years of age) (Section 366-B of IPC).

(2) The crimes identified under the Special Laws

Admittedly not all laws are gender specific, but the provisions of various laws, which affect women significantly, have been reviewed periodically and amendments carried out to keep pace with the emerging requirements. Some Acts which have special provisions to safeguard women and their interests are:

(i) Commission of Sati (Prevention) Act, 1987 (3 of 1988).

(ii) Dowry Prohibition Act, 1961 (28 of 1961).

(iii) Indecent Representation of Women (Prohibition) Act, 1986.

(iv) Immoral Traffic (Prevention) Act, 1956.

(v) Medical Termination of Pregnancy Act, 1971 (34 of 1971).

(vi) Child Marriage Restraint Act, 1929 (19 of 1929).

(vii) Hindu Marriage Act, 1955 (25 of 1955).

(viii) Hindu Succession Act, 1956 (3 of 1956).

(ix) Contract Labour (Regulation & Abolition) Act, 1970 (37 of 1970).

(x) Equal Remuneration Act, 1976 (25 of 1976).

(xi) Factories Act, 1948 (63 of 1948) as amended in 1976.

(xii) Maternity Benefit Act, 1961, (53 of 1961).

(xiii) Criminal Law (Amendment) Act, 1983.

(xiv) Special Marriage Act, 1954.

(xv) The Family Courts Act, 1954.
(xvi) Employees State Insurance Act, 1948.
(xvii) Plantation Labour Act, 1951.

STEPS TAKEN TO CURB VIOLENCE AGAINST WOMEN

Under the Constitution of India law and order is a state subject. The responsibility for dealing with enforcement of the concerned acts, therefore, rests with the state governments. The registration cases, investigation, detection and prevention of the crimes against women are primarily with state government/union territory Administrations. However, the Government of India has initiated a number of measures apart from legislative changes in the relevant acts. Instructions/guidelines have been issued to the state governments/union territory administrations to effectively enforce legislation relating to crimes against women and monitor the enforcement.

The Minister of Human Resource Development has written, during August 2000 to all State Home Ministers stressing the need for including gender sensitization modules as a component of training courses for enforcement machinery in the state level police training academies and also on the need for gender sensitization of judiciary. NGOs have been constituted to monitor the implementation of the Supreme Court's guidelines.

Various statutes exist, which recognize women specific crimes, both social and physical and the need to combat it. This has led to various proactive and preventive measures including protective legislation for women. The impact of these measures and legislation, however, requires to be strengthened. The Government has also been strengthening the existing legislations and developing new institutional machineries through extensive research and review. In addition to gender sensitization of law enforcement personnel and so forth on one hand and on the other, it has set up and running projects that provide support to vulnerable women like short stay homes, hostels for working women etc and rehabilitation of victims of violence. The Central Social

Welfare Board is implementing the scheme of Family Counselling Centres (FCCs) to provide preventive rehabilitative service to women and children who are victims of atrocities and family mal-adjustments. At present, 17 FCCs are running in district police headquarters in different states. 19 FFCs are functioning in Police Headquarters at Delhi, Kerala, West Bengal, Orissa, Tripura, Pondicherry, Assam, Karnataka, Manipur, Goa, Maharashtra, Punjab, Haryana, Meghalaya, Nagaland, Uttar Pradesh, Sikkim, Tamil Nadu and Madhya Pradesh.

In order to address the phenomenon of domestic violence, which is widely prevalent but has remained largely invisible, the Government has introduced a legislation titled 'Protection from Domestic Violence Bill, 2002' in the Lok Sabha on 8th March, 2002 to empower magistrates to grant protection orders to victims of domestic violence and provide other relief. The Bill envisages that the protection officers would assist a victim of domestic violence to be secure from violence and help her access shelter homes, health care, legal advice etc.

'Crimes Against Women's Cells' have been set up in the states of Andhra Pradesh, Punjab, Orissa, Rajasthan, Tamil Nadu, Uttar Pradesh, Himachal Pradesh, Karnataka, Madhya Pradesh and in the union territories of Chandigarh, Delhi and Pondicherry.

During the Women's Empowerment Year, 2001, the department has written to all state governments to set up district level committees headed by the district magistrates to review and monitor cases of crimes against women. State governments such as Andhra Pradesh, Chhatisgarh, Haryana, Kerala, Madhya Pradesh, Meghalaya, Mizoram, Orissa, Punjab and Uttar Pradesh have reported to set up such Committees.

The Government of India has also initiated steps to organize an effective campaign to sensitize the public about violence against women and also initiated action to compile and collate statistical information pertaining to seven types of crimes against women. These are (i) rape (Section 376 of

Indian Penal Code), (ii) causing miscarriage (Section 312 to 316), (iii) harassment, both mental and physical in a marital relationship and offences relating to marriage (Chapter XX of IPC, (iv) dowry death (Section 304 B), (v) molestation as defined by Section 354 of Indian Penal Code, (vi) kidnapping and abduction (Section 366), and (vii) procuration of minor girls (Section 366 A).

Empowerment of Women

Ultimately one of the major causes e.g., the economic dependence of women and lack of financial independence leads to atrocities against women. The need to make them economically independent has, therefore, been given utmost importance in recent schemes, projects and programmes over the past two decades. The Government has launched many schemes such as Women's Economic Programme (NORAD), Support to Training and Employment Programme (STEP), Socio-Economic Programme (SEP), Condensed Course for Vocational and Educational Training (CCE&VT) etc. for their uplift and self-sustenance.

The scheme, 'Women in Difficult Circumstances (Swadhar)' launched by the Department of Women and Child Development is an innovative approach to cater to the requirement of various types of women in distress in diverse situations under different conditions. The schemes provide shelter, counseling and training for women in difficult circumstances who do not have any social and economical support.

A social advocacy-cum-legal literacy drive through 'Education Work for Prevention of Atrocities on Women' is being implemented by the department since 1982. It provides financial assistance to voluntary organizations working for the upliftment and betterment of women and for the prevention of atrocities against women, for propaganda, publicity and research work. Production of publicity materials like pamphlets, booklets, hoardings, posters, slogans, surveys/ studies on particular aspect of violence/atrocities against women qualifies for financial assistance under this scheme.

Since 1996 the Government has sought to involve the state governments and NGOs to confer economic empowerment through the vehicle of Self Help Group formation. The Swashakti Scheme being implemented by Department of Women and Child Development, Government of India in nine states with ultimate objective of making Self help groups self sustaining units and economically viable. The economic strength, thus, garnered will enable women to understand domestic and external operations.

Legal literacy has been made part and parcel of all the programmes that have been launched by Government of India in the recent past, such as Swashakti (Rural Women's Development and Empowerment Project) and Swayamsidha.

There is also a programme to generate general awareness among the rural and poor women, the Awareness Generation Programme (AGP). The broad aim of this programme is to create awareness among the rural and poor women on various social issues so that they can realize their potential in the family and society. Since 1993-94, special emphasis is being given to the participation of women in Panchayati Raj Institutions and their role in national integration and communal harmony.

Institutional Mechanism

Department of Women and Child Development

The Department of Women and Child Development was set up in the year 1985 as a part of the Ministry of Human Resource Development to give the required impetus to the development of women and children. In its capacity as the nodal agency looking after the advancement of women and children, the department formulates plans, policies, and programmes; enacts/amends legislations affecting women and children and guides and coordinates the efforts of both governmental and non-governmental organizations working field in the of women and child development. Apart from this, the Department of Women and Child Development also implements certain innovative programmes for women and children. These programmes are in the areas of employment and income generation, welfare and support services, gender sensitization, training for employment and income generation and awareness generation.

National Commission for Women

The Government has set up a statutory body called National Commission for Women (NCW) with a specific mandate to study and monitor all matters relating to the Constitutional and legal safeguards provided to women; review the existing legislations to suggest amendments wherever necessary; and to look into complaints involving deprivation of the rights of women. NCW is receiving complaints relating to dowry/atrocity cases, dowry related suicides/death/murder etc. These cases are duly processed in the commission under Section 10(1) (f) and 10(1) (g) of the NCW Act, 1990 and referred to the appropriate authorities such as police, district magistrates etc with the Commission's recommendations for expediting action under the criminal laws and bringing the guilty persons to trial in the Court. These cases are tried in courts having criminal jurisdiction under Sections 304-B, 498-A, 302 etc. of the Indian Penal Code. NCW has conducted Parivarik Mahila Lok Adalats as a form of alternate dispute resolution with the help of NGOs and Legal Aid Boards at state and district levels to facilitate access to law enforcement systems and faster justice delivery to poor women in case of family dispute, dowry harassment etc.

Immediately after enactment of National Commission for Women Act, 1990 on 31st August, 1990, the Government had, by way of D.O letter dated 30.10.90 from the then Minister for Labour and Welfare, requested the chief ministers of all state governments to consider constitution of State level Women Commissions with functions and powers similar to that of NCW. Since then, the government has been requesting the state governments to set up State level Women Commissions. D.O letters at the level of Minister-in-charge of the Ministry of Human Resource Development/Department of Women and Child Development have been issued on 22.2.93, 24.8.95, 25.10.96, 4.6.99 and on 20.8.2001. The issue of setting up of State Women Commissions is also taken up with the state governments/union territory administrations during the meetings held by the Government periodically with state ministers and secretaries-in-charge of Women & Child Development.

Central Social Welfare Board

The Central Social Welfare Board (CSWB) is an apex national organization involved in programmes for the welfare and development of women, children and disadvantaged groups. The Central Social Welfare Board was set up in 1953. with the objective of facilitating a bridge between government and the voluntary sector in the country to reach benefits of Government schemes to the backward sections of our society. At present, the CSWB is engaged in supporting thousands of voluntary organizations all over the country to implement programmes for disadvantaged groups of women and children.

Rashtriya Mahila Kosh

The National Credit Fund for women called Rashtriya Mahila Kosh (RMK) is a poverty alleviation strategy, which is using the Self-Help Group concept successfully. RMK is poised to expand, with support from the national budget to its corpus fund, its loaning programme from the present level of about Rs. 190 million to Rs. 1000 million per year by March, 2003 and will be catering to a variety of micro-credit needs of about half a million borrowers.

National Institute of Public Cooperation and Child Development (NIPCCD)

Since 1986, a separate Women's Development Division has been functioning in the Institute. The Institute has been sensitizing enforcement machineries, training NGOs and pursuing legal advocacy and literacy. It has been acting as a Lead Training Agency (LTA) for 'Swashakti' and is Lead Agency for implementing 'Swayamsidha' which aims to make rural women economically independent giving them strength to combat violence against them.

Parliamentary Committee on Empowerment of Women

A Parliament Committee on Empowerment of Women has been constituted in 1997 for considering the reports of the National Commission for Women, to examine the measure taken by the government to secure women's equality and to report on the working of welfare programmes for women etc.

Non-Governmental Organizations

In India, NGOs and umbrella organizations are powerful and active agents in gender advocacy and training. In areas such as women's rights, economic and political empowerment of women and violence against women, the contribution of voluntary sector and the government's collaboration with them have brought about positive results. Increase of women in parliamentary and local government levels has come about as a result of government policies including legislations, ably supported by NGO advocacy. The NGOs in India have taken up a number of programmes to prepare women to contest elections and occupy elected positions.

The CSWB acts as an umbrella organization networking through State Welfare Boards and through them thousand of voluntary organizations.

Future Programmes

Action Plan for implementing the National Policy for Empowerment of Women

The Government of India has adopted a National Policy for the Empowerment of Women. The goal of the Policy is to bring about the advancement, development and empowerment of women by creating an environment through positive social and economic policies and programmes for development of women in all spheres of life. Para 7.1 of the Policy lays down as under:

7.1 Institutions and mechanisms/schemes for assistance will be created and strengthened for prevention of such violence including sexual harassment at work place and customs like dowry; for the rehabilitation of the victims of violence and for taking effective action against the perpetrators of such violence. A special emphasis will also be laid on programmes and measures to deal with trafficking in women and girls.

The Government is drafting a National Plan of Action (POA) to implement the National Policy for the Empowerment of Women. The POA will focus on creating support infrastructure to compliment legislative efforts, creating a conducive environment to women for reporting cases related to violence against them. Gender sensitivity among the policy makers will be strengthened along with awareness on the prevention of atrocities on women.

Enactment of Protection from Domestic Violence Bill, 2002

In order to address the phenomenon of domestic violence which is widely prevalent but has remained largely invisible in the public domain, a legislation titled 'Protection from Domestic Violence Bill, 2002' has been introduced in Lok Sabha on 8th March, 2002 to empower courts to grant protection orders to victims of domestic violence and provide other relief. The Bill has been referred to the Parliamentary Standing Committee attached to the Ministry of Human Resources Development for examination and report.

Drafting of Bill on sexual harassment at workplace

The Supreme Court of India, in its judgment dated 13.8.97 in a civil writ petition, laid down detailed guidelines to be followed by employers at all working places to prevent sexual harassment of women. The guidelines, inter-alia, stipulate that committees will be set up by each employer to handle complaints of sexual harassment. In accordance with the guidelines laid down by the Supreme Court, the government has initiated action to constitute complaints committees in all ministries/departments of the central as well as state governments, public sector undertakings etc. So far 58 ministries/departments of Government of India and 24 state governments and union territory administrations have reported setting up of complaints committees. The Central Civil Services (Conduct) Rules have been amended to include sexual harassment as a prohibited conduct. In order to ensure implementation of the guidelines in the private sector, Industrial Employment (Standing Orders) Act, 1946 has been amended.

The National Commission for Women is drafting legislation relating to prevention of sexual harassment of women at workplace.

2

Crime and Violence Against Women : The Situation in Assam

Trend, Dimension, Police Action and Societal Reaction

Dr. Archana Sharma
Ms. Indranoshee Das

Introduction

Home sweet home; there is no place like home. But what happens when your own home turns out to be a prison? What happens when your own near and dear ones turn your worst enemy? What happens when you know your enemy, but have to live and tolerate him lest you should be blamed, lest your action should be termed blasphemous? What happens when you are forced to learn some truths of life well ahead of time, so much so that even chocolate turns bitter before you can taste its sweetness? Yes, this is what happens to hundreds and thousands of women in our country. To use National Family Health Survey statistics, one out of every five Indian women and one out of every seven women in Assam, face one or the other form of domestic violence. In majority of the cases of domestic violence, the perpetrator is none other than the husband, yes, the husband with whom she had taken the sacred oath of remaining together through thick and thin, throughout her life, until death. Yes, the 'Husband' who is supposed to give her shelter, love and respect! And, she is not supposed to tell anyone about it, for she is beaten for her fault, yes, she deserves that because may be she had not cooked properly, may be she does not have a male child, may be she has not been attentive to her children and there can be many more such trivial reasons, but there is nothing wrong in beating a wife, at least that is what two out of every three women believe. Or were they taught to believe? In fact, in most societies domestic violence against women is not perceived as a crime. It is seen as a matter of individual responsibility. In most cases, the perpetrators get acceptance in the society while the victim continues to be looked down upon, as if she herself was responsible for her plight. The victim has no other way but to suffer in silence. (ICRW, May 2002, *Domestic Violence in India: Exploring Strategies, Promoting Dialogue*.)

Women in Indian society have been victims of ill treatment, humiliation, torture and exploitation as long as written records of social organization and family life are available. But regretfully, female victims of violence have not been given much attention in the literature on criminal violence. (Ahuja R, 1998) The attitude of indifference and negligence can be attributed to factors like general acceptance of man's superiority over women because of which violent acts against women were not viewed as violent or deviant and the denial of violence by women themselves owing to their socio-cultural values and attitudes.

Violence has surrounded a women's life from birth to death and has become a routinized affair in all societies of the world since innumerable centuries. A narrow concept of violence may suggest an act of illegal criminal use of physical force, but it also includes exploitation, discrimination, upholding of an unequal economic and social structure, creation of an atmosphere of terror, a situation of threat reprisal and other forms of political violence (Sinha N, 1989).

Violence runs along the lines of power in the sex/gender system. Still more agonizing is the failure of the control system in modern India due to which the intensity, frequency and type of violence against women are increasing day by day. Many victims cannot face endless, time consuming litigation. A timely visit by the police would do wonders... But we dare not trust them. (*The Hindu*, Oct.9, 2002). Violent incidents are so numerous that no eyebrows are raised when a new incident is added to the long list. Crimes against women seem never ending.

Crime against women in India is broadly classified under two categories: 1. crimes identified under the Indian Penal Code (IPC) and 2. crimes identified under the special laws (SL). The crimes under the former category include eight types:

- Rape (section 376 IPC)
- Kidnapping and abduction (sections 363 and 373)
- Dowry homicides (section 302 and 304 B)
- Torture-physical and mental (section 498 A)
- Molestation (section 354)
- Eve-teasing or sexual harassment (section 509)
- Importation of girls (section 366 B) and
- Murder (other than dowry homicides) (section 302).

The crimes under the latter category include four types:

- Immoral trafficking (1956 Act)
- Demanding dowry (1961 Act)
- Commission of *Sati* (1987 Act), and
- Indecent representation of women (1986 Act). (Ahuja R, 1998)

Domestic violence cannot be eliminated altogether. The incidence of domestic violence against women is the highest among all the forms of violence, where the perpetrator being none other than someone known to the victim, someone closes to the family, someone near and dear to the victim. Many such cases go unreported out of fear that the victim and the victim's family will be castigated and/or alienated from the society. With increased awareness about women's rights and the changing gender concepts under the influence of feminist thinking, there has, however, been a change in the societal outlook towards such incidents. The intervention of women's organizations, social workers and NGOs also has contributed to such positive changes.

Various UN agencies have been highlighting as well as raising their voice against the worldwide trend of violence against women. In India not only is wife beating a common practice but also three out of every five women (56 per cent) believe that wife beating is justified for six specific reasons. The NFHS -2 has revealed that 40 per cent of the women agreed that neglecting the house or children justified the thrashing. Other commonly accepted justifications include the wife going out without telling the husband (37 %); the wife showing disrespect for in-laws (34 %) and the wife being unfaithful (33 %). Less acceptable reasons include the wife not cooking the food properly (25 %) and the woman's parents not giving expected money, jewellery or other items (7 %).

The Domestic Violence (Prevention) Bill is a significant step forward in recognizing the problems of women, children and other family members living in an atmosphere of violence. When it is finally enacted, it will provide protection against domestic violence by obtaining protection, residence and monetary relief orders. *The Protection from Domestic Violence Bill suffers from a number of defects. One of them is that it does not provide a clear and comprehensive definition of domestic violence, and leaves much to the discretion of individual judges. (The Hindu, Aug 04, 2002)* There is more to domestic violence than physical abuse. Emotional trauma can be far more crippling and a new bill seeks to recognize that. (*The Week*, Feb 03, 2002).

Crimes against women can be studied under three clusters - social, personal and psychological and legal. (Saxena S, 1995). Social causes include causes like inferior status of women due to social conditioning, patriarchal structure of society, lack of proper training, broken homes, too much interference by parents, etc. "Men are consciously taught to be aggressive and tough while women are conditioned to be submissive and docile".

Objectives

The objectives of the present paper are to find out:

- Dimension and trend in the incidence of crime and violence against women in India with special reference to Assam.

a) The inter-district pattern in crime and violence against women in Assam.

b) Action/inaction of the lawmakers and the societal reaction to such incidents.

Coverage

The paper covers a period of six years from 1997 to 2002. For inter district analysis, all the 23 districts of Assam has been included.

Methodology

The paper uses both analytical and descriptive methods. Quantitative techniques like finding out simple percentages as well as more rigorous techniques like regression equations and curve fitting on the basis of linear regression analysis also have been used.

Data Source

The paper depends largely on primary source of data - the source from the office of the DIG, CID, Assam. National Family Health Survey -II have also been used.

For the case studies, newspaper reports have been used.

The Crime Situation in India

Like most offences, Crime Against Women (CAW) is steadily on the rise in India. Of the total crimes reported in the country seven percent constitute CAW. The all-India rate, number of crimes per 100, 000 population reported to the police, was 13.8 during 1999. This may not be alarming at first sight but the point is many crimes are not reported. Hideous forms of violence in the subcontinent prove that women are still powerless. (*The Hindu,* July 14, 2002)

Violence against women and the girl children, both domestic and at the workplace has been showing an alarming trend. As per the data (1999) published by the National Crime Records Bureau, New Delhi, the total number of crimes committed against women has been increasing year by year from 1.21 lakh in 1997 to 1.31 lakh in 1998 and 1.36 lakh in 1999. Of the total 1.36 lakh crimes against women in 1999, torture claims the highest share of 32.3%, followed by molestation (23.8%), kidnapping and abduction (11.7%), rape (11.4%), sexual harassment (6.5%) and dowry death (4.9%, immoral traffic (6.9%) and others (2.5%).

Amongst the states, while Madhya Pradesh reports the highest incidence of 12.6 % of the total crimes, Uttar Pradesh and Maharashtra followed suit with 12.5 % and 10% respectively. (Five Year Plan, 2002-2007, Volume II)

Of the 23 big cities, Chennai accounted for 21.2 per cent followed by Delhi at 12 per cent. Among the six metros, Kolkata is the safest for women. As much as 31.2 per cent of dowry deaths were from Uttar Pradesh alone, followed by Bihar with 15.2 per cent. But incidence of torture accounted for 12.3 percent in UP and only 3.2 per cent of cases reported in Bihar. Harassment for dowry is noticed only when the authorities are confronted with bodies of the helpless women. In cases of rape, victims knew the offenders in 84 of every 100 cases. Neighbours were accused of rape in three of every 10 cases. The aspirations of a woman trapped in a murderous marriage and seeking relief from its bondage do not find reflection in any of our laws. Irretrievable breakdown of marriage is not a ground for divorce in India. Courts also use archaic methods to settle disputes over custody of children, marital property, return of *streedhan*, maintenances that often weigh heavily against the interests of the woman.

One in every five murders in 1999 was of women. Personal enmity, property disputes, love intrigues, dowry and gain are the major reasons for murdering women. Kidnapping and abduction of women account for 67 per cent of the 23,864 cases reported. A significant feature is that 54 per cent of the victims were less than 18 years old.

The failure of the investigating agency can be seen from the fact that 36 per cent of the cases remained under investigation, without finalization, till the end of the year. These are cases in which victims remained untraced or the investigation was under way to establish the charge. The police closed as many as 4,229 cases of kidnapping and abduction as false, mistake of fact or law. This signifies the shifting stand taken by the victim or her family towards the crime and the criminal in view of the existing social environment.

The number of sexual harassment cases, referred to as eve teasing in the past, rose by 10 per cent in 1999. More than 25 per cent of these cases were reported from Uttar Pradesh, followed by Tamil Nadu and Andhra Pradesh contributing 20 per cent each. It is natural to expect a significant co-relation in the pattern of rape, molestation and sexual harassment cases reported from a State. But, this pattern is not reflected in the statistics. Madhya Pradesh recorded the largest number of rape and molestation cases but ranks much lower in the reporting of sexual harassment cases. The reason for Uttar Pradesh recording far lesser number of rapes and molestation cases than other States but recording the highest number of sexual harassment cases is an issue for serious study. This is suggestive of the failure of the criminal justice system to inspire confidence in the victims and their inability to speak out. It also raises serious doubts about the correct recording of cases as they occur and the shocking apathy to gender issues.

The significantly large number of sexual harassment cases reported from Tamil Nadu and Andhra Pradesh are perhaps a pointer to the drive taken up by these States against gender crimes.

A study of the figures of cases reported under the Immoral Traffic (Prevention) Act implies that prostitution thrives in Tamil Nadu, Andhra Pradesh and Karnataka as 90 per cent of the cases have been reported from here. (*The Hindu,* Sept., 01, 2002, Tejdeep Kaur Menon, *Inspector General of Police, Special Protection Force, Andhra Pradesh.)*

The high incidence of dowry deaths, torture or cruel treatment of women in northern India including Delhi and some Union Territories such as Chandigarh, Daman and Diu, Dadra and Nagar Haveli, and Andaman and Nicobar Islands may all be contributing factors leading to relatively shorter life spans among adult women. Better sex ratios are noted among the southern states, some hill regions and in states where tribal groups are a significant proportion of the population.

Crime situation in Assam : An Analysis

Because of an actual increase in the crime rate, the number of reported cases of crime and violence against women has increased considerably all over the country during the last decade. The North East and Assam are no exception. Mizoram recorded the highest and Arunachal Pradesh recorded third highest in rape rate in India during 1991 to 1997, and in both the states it is still rising. Assam is following the pattern of Mizoram at lower level. Molestation rate in Sikkim, Tripura and Mizoram is higher than the national average throughout the reference period; however, there is constant decline in Tripura whereas Nagaland remained at lowest level in the region. Assam and Arunachal Pradesh have the kidnapping and abduction rate quite higher than the level of national average; however, in Manipur it is declining constantly. Contrary to this, Assam has shown constant upward trend. Except Mizoram, all other states are having total cognizable crime rate below the national level. Manipur showed constant decline whereas, Assam showed opposite trend and is rising at much faster rate than the national increase rate. (Pralip Narzary's paper on *Crime against Women in North East India,* submitted in the National Seminar on Women in the North East: Challenges and Opportunities for the 21st Century organized by the WSRC, Gauhati University)

Insurgency, internal conflicts, societal structure, political instability, lax administrative control, increasing poverty and lack of proper economic development are identified as the roots of growing social evils of the region. These evils also include the increased incidence of crime and violence against women. It is, however, paradoxical and very pathetic that the region, where even today women have a much higher rate of autonomy than their counterparts in the rest of the Country is attracting attention for having high rate of violence against women.

An analysis of the data for the state and for her 23 districts reveal that during the period 1997-2002, there has not only been an increase in the number of crimes and violence against women in Assam(Table 2.1 and 2.2) , but also the incidence of crime is well spread over all the districts. Crime rates were, however, much higher in some of the districts. Overall crime rate in the State has increased by approximately 36 per cent over the period.

Among the different forms of crime, total case of kidnapping is the highest followed by cruelty by husband and rape. Dowry deaths comprise a small percentage of total crimes. On the contrary, the rate of increase over time in dowry death and that of cruelty by husband are alarmingly high, whereas the rate of increase in kidnapping is much lower. Another form of crime that had increased at a galloping rate is immoral trafficking. The different forms of crime recorded, viz., kidnapping, rape, molestation, cruelty by husband, dowry death and immoral traffic rates increased by 10.42%, 23.29%, 09.91%, 101.29%, 181.81% and 100.0% respectively (Table 2.2).

Table 2.1
CRIME AND VIOLENCE AGAINST WOMEN IN ASSAM: 1997-2002*

Year	Type of Crime						
	Kidnapping	Rape	Molestation	Cruelty by husband	Dowry death	Immoral traffic	Total
1997	1113	717	686	775	22	10	3323
1998	1117	744	648	739	32	12	3292
	(+4)	(+27)	(-38)	(-36)	(+10)	(+02)	(-31)
1999	1149	703	720	843	40	9	3464
	(+32)	(-41)	(+72)	(+104)	(+08)	(-03)	(+172)
2000	1101	762	777	978	50	15	3683
	(-48)	(+59)	(+57)	(+135)	(+10)	(+06)	(+219)
2001	1070	817	850	1248	59	4	4048
	(-31)	(+55)	(+73)	(+270)	(+09)	(-11)	(+365)
2002	1229	884	754	1560	62	20	4509
	(+159)	(+67)	(-96)	(+312)	(+03)	(16)	(+461)
Total increase/decrease from 1997-2002	116 (10.42)	167 (23.29)	68 (09.91)	785 (101.29)	40 (181.81)	10 (100.0)	1186 (35.69)

Note : Figures in parentheses in rows 2 to 6 show increase/decrease over the previous year, figures in brackets in row 7 shows percentage increase/decrease between 1997 and 2002.

* *Source:* Office of the DIG, CID, Assam.

Looking at the inter district differences (Table 2.3) in the crime rate; it has been observed that all forms of crime had an increasing rate in all the 23 districts. Kamrup, Cachar and Nagaon happened to be the three worst districts in terms of crime against women, followed by Sonitpur and Dhubri. With respect to rape cases, Kamrup is immediately followed by Sonitpur, while in case of dowry deaths Cachar leads, followed by Barpeta and Kamrup. Incidence of immoral trafficking is negligible elsewhere but as high as 44 in Kamrup. The cultural pattern of the particular district, the rate of urbanization and growth rate of slums seemed to have an influence in the inter district pattern of the crimes. The high rates of crime in the districts like Sonitpur and Dhubri and to some extent Nagaon may also be attributed to insurgency.

Table 2.2

PERCENTAGE DISTRIBUTION OF CRIME AND VIOLENCE AGAINST WOMEN IN ASSAM: 1997-2002*

Year	Types of Crime						
	Kidnapping	Rape	Molestation	Cruelty by husband	Dowry death	Immoral traffic	Total
1997	33.50	21.58	20.64	23.32	0.66	0.30	100
1998	33.93	22.60	19.68	22.45	0.97	0.36	100
1999	33.17	20.29	20.79	24.34	1.15	0.26	100
2000	29.89	20.69	21.10	26.55	1.36	0.41	100
2001	26.43	20.18	20.99	30.83	1.46	0.10	100
2002	27.26	19.61	16.72	34.60	1.38	0.44	100
Total	30.37	20.73	19.87	27.52	1.19	0.31	100

* **Source**: Estimated from Table 2.1.

Another form of crime affecting more women than men that has already taken serious proportions in some of the tribal dominated districts is that of witch hunting. Data on this form of violence is not separately shown in the police records. In some tribal dominated pockets in the districts of Goalpara, Bongaigaon, Kokrajhar, Nalbari and Dhubri districts, some women are identified as witches and believed that because of her presence in the village, the village community suffers from diseases and other problems. So, she is driven away from the village, beheaded, beaten to death, punished and tortured in many ways as possible. Sometimes her husband and the family also get into trouble if they continue to protect her. It is yet to be established whether this is due to some blind belief and superstition or it is linked to some personal /professional rivalry or linked to insurgency.

Table 2.3

TOTAL NO. OF DIFFERENT FORMS OF CRIME AGAINST WOMEN IN ASSAM BY DISTRICTS, 1997-2002

SL. No.	District	Kidnapping	Rape	Molestation	Cruelty by husband	Dowry death	Immmoral traffic	Total	% share of each district
1	Bongaigaon	165	115	122	150	8	0	560	2.51
2	Dhemaji	139	212	148	177	2	0	678	3.04
3	Sonitpur	472	**329**	221	365	**21**	5	1413	**6.33**
4	Goalpara	144	149	139	248	2	2	684	3.07
5	Jorhat	203	173	149	192	2	2	721	3.23
6	Nagaon	**765**	**327**	**611**	**477**	**15**	2	**2197**	**9.84**
7	Hailakandi	200	122	198	152	9	0	681	3.05
8	Kamrup	**1002**	**431**	491	**459**	**32**	**44**	**2459**	**11.02**
9	Darrang	261	242	292	150	21	0	966	4.33
10	Barpeta	325	292	179	438	**33**	1	1268	5.68
11	Dhubri	290	250	285	**569**	17	2	1413	**6.33**
12	Nalbari	180	133	122	80	5	1	521	2.33
13	Morigaon	181	134	124	129	6	1	575	2.58

contd.

14	Dibrugarh	261	199	171	140	7	1	779	3.49
15	Lakhimpur	356	**306**	219	304	1	5	1191	5.34
16	Cachar	**538**	249	**345**	**1121**	**40**	0	**2293**	**10.28**
17	Kokrajhar	99	92	132	126	6	1	456	2.05
18	N.C. Hills	27	14	21	12	3	0	77	0.35
19	Golaghat	245	193	97	132	1	1	669	2.99
20	Karbi Anglong	117	51	73	35	8	0	284	1.27
21	Karimgunj	126	184	38	342	16	0	706	3.16
22	Tinsukia	263	202	98	142	4	1	710	3.18
23	Sivsagar	417	228	160	203	6	1	1015	4.55

Source: Office of the DIG, CID, Assam

As stated above, in all the 23 districts, crime rate has shown an increasing trend. However, it is to be noted that in certain years, 1997-2003, the rate has been alarmingly high in some districts.

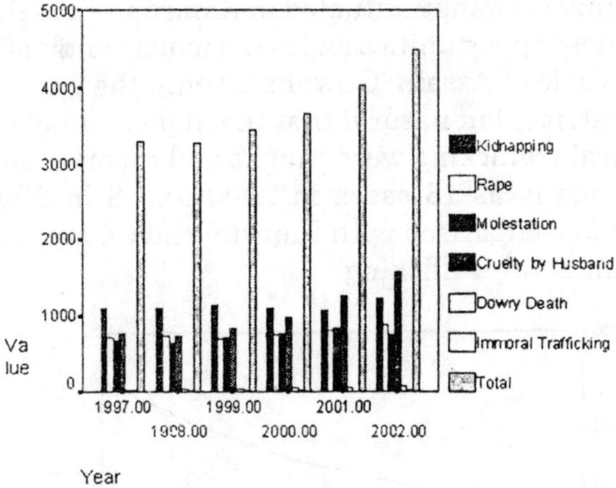

Fig. 2.1 : Crime Against Women in Assam: By Type, 1997-2002

Bongaingaon district tops the list in kidnapping with as many as 38 cases reported in 2000. Increasingly, the rate declined to 22 in 2001 while it again increased to 29 in 2002. This trend may be attributed to insurgency and other related problems. Cases reported in crimes like rape, molestation, cruelty by husband in the said district have more or less shown an upward trend. But a single case of immoral trafficking was reported in the period, 1997-2002. The year 2000 records the highest number of dowry deaths. Significantly, it is to be noted that highest number of crimes were reported in Bongaigaon district in the year 2000.

In Dhemaji, rape cases reported have shown an increasing trend, 1997-2002, while molestation cases show a declining trend. For dowry deaths and immoral trafficking, the number of cases registered is minimal.

In Sonitpur district, crimes against women in kidnapping, rape, molestation, cruelty by husband, dowry deaths and immoral trafficking have shown a more or less increasing trend in the years 1997-2002.

Kamrup being one of the most densely populated districts also shows an upward trend in crimes against women. Perhaps one of the significant reasons may be attributed to the fact that Guwahati, situated in Kamrup, offers the highest employment opportunities and is the major centre of activities for the whole of Assam. Guwahati being the gateway of the north east, it is but natural that the highest number of cases of immoral trafficking were caught and reported in Kamrup with as many as 13 cases in 2000 and 8 in 2002. Other districts in comparison with Kamrup show a minimal rate in case of immoral trafficking.

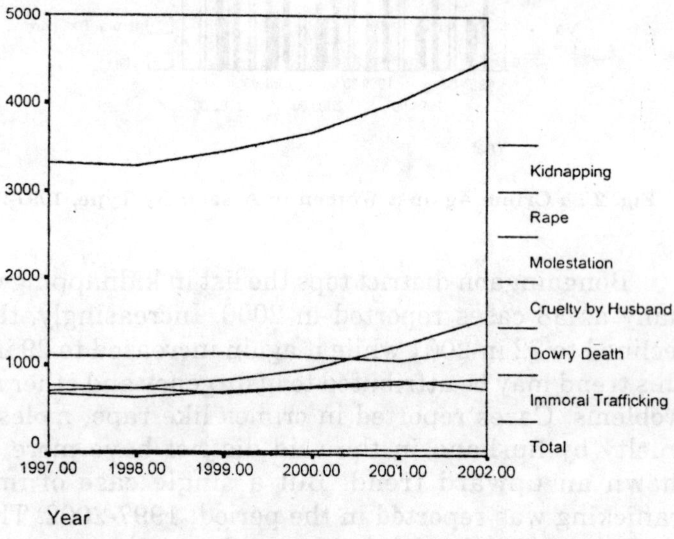

Fig. 2.2 : Trend of Crimes Against Women in Assam: By Type, 1997-2002

Another densely populated district, Nagaon also shows the same increasing trend in crime against women. The rates are significantly higher for kidnapping, rape, molestation, and cruelty by husband.

Jorhat, one of the most literate districts of Assam shows the absence of dowry deaths. Not a single case of dowry death was reported in the period considered, 1997 - 2002.

North Cachar hills, being a sparsely populated district apparently shows the least number of crimes against women. *(Office of the DIG, CID, Assam)*

The data and the accompanying graphs can very well make one feel how horrifying the present situation is! The state and the community, which used to announce with pride that *our women are better off because we do not have the dowry system; instead some of our communities have to pay a bride price,* now find that dowry deaths have increased by nearly 200 (181.81%) in six years. The steep curves/trend lines in the case of each form of crime make one feel more concern about the issue.

However, the data show only the magnanimity of the problem in the form of some quantities and it does not carry the agony of the sufferer. If the plight of the actual victims is not understood, sometimes, these data may become mere lifeless statistics lacking a human face and hence very comfortably forgotten by policymakers as the policy makers have a tendency to rank the problems in terms of quantities only, the higher the number, the more the attention. This is feared because if looked at as mere numbers, 255 numbers of dowry deaths, i.e., an average of 62.5 such cases per year may not sound too big in the face of increasing incidence of all forms of crime in police records; hence this may very well remain out of the purview of the policy makers. It has, in fact been observed even responsible police officers cannot find any reason why there should be so much commotion about this particular issue whereas increase in the overall crime rate has become commonplace. Even the counselors in Legal Aid Cells have a tendency to tackle cases of cruelty by the husband by first asking the victim, what had she done, she must have done something to provoke his anger, she must have been intolerant. As if, they believe if the husband is displeased, he can give her a beating. This may be because of the mindset framed by the traditional patriarchal society, where domestic violence against women is taken to be the husband's right and also because of a tendency to ignore a problem as long as it is possible, so that they do not get into more trouble by tackling it. Sometimes it is also wrongly believed that these incidents occur among the uneducated and the poor, and these are their daily bread, such things do not happen in respectable families, (which undoubtedly is a myth). Sometimes, even before knowing the complete story, prior judgments about the women's character, behaviour etc. are formed and the justice to be given to the women is delayed and/or denied. Loopholes in existing law of the land also sometimes stand on the way of justice to the victim.

All this also casts heavy responsibility on women police already saddled with important tasks and issues relating to search, arrest, custody of women witnesses, arrestees and juvenile delinquents. But there is just one policewoman for every 45 policemen, a woefully inadequate 2.09 per cent of the entire police force.

As many as 18 states have strength of less than 1,000 each. Maharashtra is in the lead with 4,345 police women. The share of women in armed police is 0.39 per cent. They exist only in a few states - Madhya Pradesh, Himachal Pradesh, Jammu and Kashmir, Assam, Goa and Delhi. There are not enough police women for investigation.

• Rape by officials as well as private individuals constitutes an act of torture for which the state must be held to account when it has failed to fulfil its obligation to provide effective protection. The few women who have had the courage to bring charges of sexual violence are reported to have found the police, health, rehabilitation and justice systems utterly unresponsive to their needs, with staff backing each other in negating the gravity of sexual abuses.

In many cases, victims were requested to file complaints with the same police officers who allegedly colluded with their abusers, and who reportedly refused to record their statements or did so in a defective manner.

In the few cases of rape, which have reached to the courts, priority is reportedly given to the prosecution of offences of murder over those of rape, when the two happened during the same incident. The result is that perpetrators of rape are often not prosecuted. Medical reports continue to be requested by courts as a paramount piece of corroborative evidence in the prosecution of rape cases. In many cases, however, survivors of sexual violence were unable to access the health system after being abused, while bodies of raped women were often burnt by the attackers, in order to destroy the evidence of their crime. Requesting victims to produce medical reports often amounts to complying with the perpetrators' strategy.

In such a situation, there is no question of police women being available to tackle cases where the woman is the victim rather than the offender. It is time to put on the thinking caps. (*The Hindu* Sunday, Sept. 01, 2002, Tejdeep Kaur Menon, *Inspector General of Police, Special Protection Force, Andhra Pradesh.)*

POLICE ACTION : *THE SCENARIO IN ASSAM*

The ready statistics on crime and violence against women provided by the police is one example of their concern. In order to tackle crime involving women, a Special Cell for monitoring and co-ordinating investigation of cases of crimes against women and immoral traffic have been functioning in the C.I.D. since 1994 under the direct supervision of the DIG(CID), Assam, Guwahati. This Cell has been doggedly supervising all the important cases all over the State involving crime against women. Thorough supervision, constant monitoring and progress of investigation of offences like dowry death, rape, immoral trafficking in women keep the Cell busy.

In the recent years, C.I.D. has taken over investigation of 20 cases of physical violence against women and successfully investigated the same. Realizing its commitment to the society, this Cell has resolved to curb social menaces like prostitution and dowry deaths. The cell has also conducted raids in hotels, restaurants, private houses, beauty parlours etc. and arrested many offenders to book.

This Cell has been instrumental in setting up a Family Counseling Centre at the C.I.D. HQ since 15th September 1997 in consultation with the Social Welfare Department. So far, the counseling Centre has taken up 91 cases, of which it has been able to sort out marital discord in 60 cases.

Recently Assam Police has launched the *PROJECT PRAHARI* to deal with the problem of Witch Hunting. Another project, ASHWAS is currently working under the Assam Police to provide support to the women and children in the insurgency affected areas. They are increasing their contact and discussions with the public and the intellectuals to get societal support for tackling such problems.

As against this gleam picture, there are rays of hope, for the police seem to have awakened to the problem. While the picture at the macro level is quite encouraging, reports from the field level regarding police action in such cases are somewhat mixed. The police are blamed to be reluctant to lodge even the FIR in most of the cases, particularly if the accused is some influential person. They are also alleged to be indulging in corrupt practices enabling the culprits to go unpunished; sometimes they themselves are reported to be involved in such crime. For example,

- On the 19th November 2002, a young tribal girl was raped by one police constable and Village Defence personnel. The victim accused that even the officer-in-charge of that police station knew about the incident. The incident occurred in Nagaon district. (*Sâdin*, An Assamese Weekly, Guwahati, 29th November 2002, page 23).
- In another incident, a five-year-old child was raped by a person above fifty years of age on 19th October 2002, in a police station in Kamrup district. Allegedly the accused was allowed to go scot-free for a bribe of Rs. 1400. (*Ibid*)

On the contrary there are also many instances of very efficient and commendable police action. For example:

- On 7th June, 2003, the police rescued a young married lady who was stranded at a place along the National Highway 31. The police, on interrogation, came to learn that she has been tortured by her husband for dowry. Thereafter she was sent away from her home with one of her brothers-in -law. She went from place to place with him for more than fifteen days and stayed at the places of different relatives all those days. On 7th June, they left her alone at a place not known to her. The police found her. After listening to her story, they made arrangements to send her to her own hometown. (*Âmâr Axom*, An Assamese Daily, Guwahati, 9 June, 2003)
- On 18th May, 2003, a married woman was reported to have attempted suicide by burning herself and got heavily burnt. Her husband took her to the civil hospital but she succumbed to her injuries. Thereafter, an FIR was lodged by the brother of the deceased alleging the incident to be a case of murder and not suicide. The police started the inquiry immediately and succeeded in finding sufficient evidence to prove that her husband murdered the woman. The husband was arrested. All this was done by the police within only three weeks. (*Ibid.*)

SOCIETAL REACTION

The much publicized and sensational Barnali case bears ample evidence of the ordeal through which such victims have to pass in the quest for justice. At the same time, the case also proves how societal reaction can be of great help in speeding up action. In this horrifying case of rape and murder of a little girl of nine years immediately created a furor among the public. The incident occurred at midnight in the premises of a travel agency, where the little girl was staying overnight with her parents on their way to Dimapur. The culprits were none other than four employees of the Travel Agency. Different organisations viz., the All India Democratic Women's

Asociation, Axom Mahila Sangha, Progressive Women's Association, YMCA, Pradeshik Mahila Samity etc. appealed to the Lawyers' Association not to plead for the accused. These organisations particularly the AIDWA continuously fought for punishing the culprits and giving adequate compensation to the parents of the victim. They could create sufficient pressure on all concerned. As a result, the parents of the victim were given some compensation, although it was much smaller than what was demanded. As to the punishment of the culprits, there was strong demand for capital punishment, but as is obvious, nothing beyond the law of the land can be done. This incident occurred on 13th July, 2002.In spite of so much efforts, it took nearly one year for the victim's family to get the compensation. By this time, the parents had undergone so much pain that Barnali's mother became senseless while the hearing of the Barnali case was going on in the court. (*Asomiyâ Pratidin*, 16 July, 2002, *Âmâr Axom*, 8 April, 2003)

- After the Barnali case, a number of such cases of rape of minor girls occurred. All those cases could not attract as much public attention. However, everywhere the public had expressed moral support to the victim and her family and wherever possible intervened to speed up justice. The police had also done their duty within the framework of law. But alas! Such incidents have now become routine. Newspapers carry one story after the other about violence against women. If it is rape of a minor girl today, tomorrow it may be a dowry death, the next day it may be news on immoral trafficking of young girls. So many girls have been missing, so many have been found in Mumbai or Delhi or elsewhere. As if there is never an end to these stories. Sometimes, it is felt that these news items do not have any positive value; they only create sensation and increase the sale of the paper. At the same time, it must also be admitted that without such publicity, perhaps the awareness and concern for the problem would not have been created.

REGRESSION RESULTS OF DIFFERENT TYPES OF CRIME AGAINST WOMEN IN ASSAM OVER TIME, 1997-2002

Independent: YEAR

Dependent	Mth	Rsq	d.f.	F	Sigf	b0	b1
KIDNAPPING	LIN	145	4	.68	.456	-21207	**11.1714**
RAPE	LIN	.762	4	12.78	.023	-62813	**31.8000**
MOLESTATION	LIN	.565	4	5.19	.085	-56561	**28.6571**
CRUELTY BY							
HUSBAND	**LIN**	**.865**	**4**	**25.61**	**.007**	**-318153**	159.629
Dowry Death	**LIN**	**.984**	**4**	**253.28**	**.000**	**-16580**	8.3143
IMMORAL							
TRAFFICKING	LIN	.098	4	.43	.546	-1816.4	**.9143**
TOTAL	LIN	.890	4	32.20	.005	-477131	**240.486**

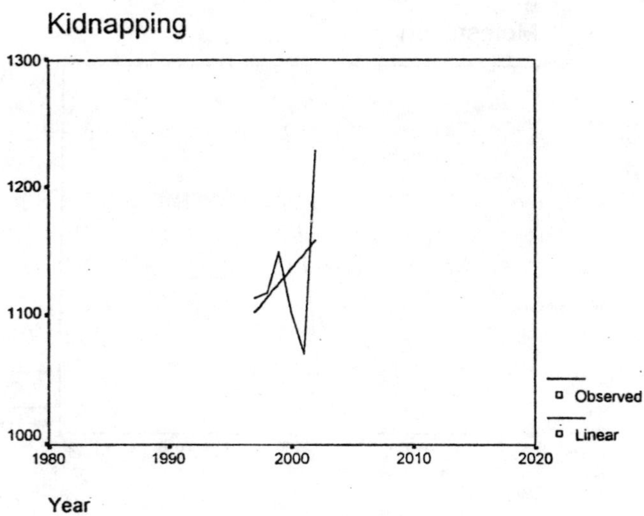

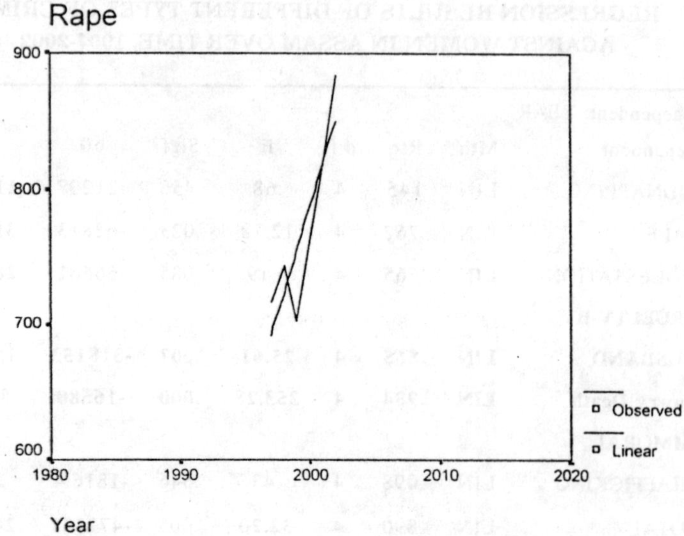
Rape
900
800
700
600
1980
1990
2000
2010
2020
Year
Observed
Linear

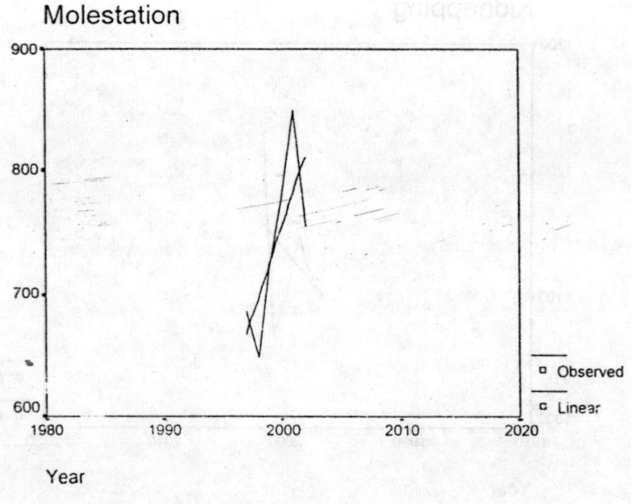
Molestation
900
800
700
600
1980
1990
2000
2010
2020
Year
Observed
Linear

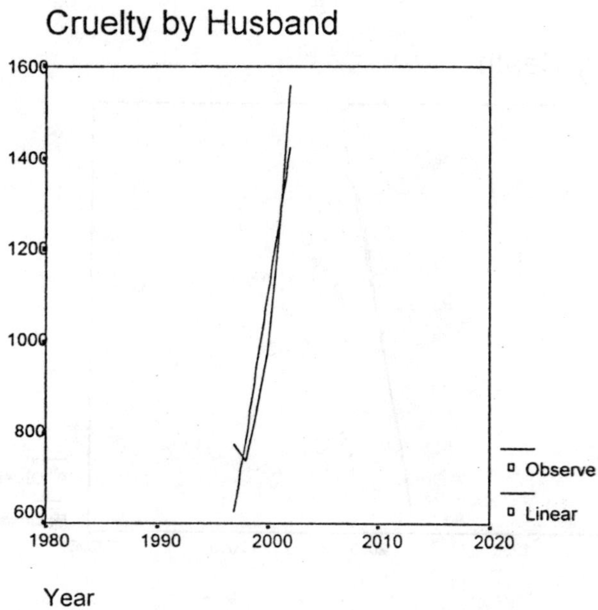
Cruelty by Husband
1600
1400
1200
1000
800
600
1980
1990
2000
2010
2020
Year
Observe
Linear

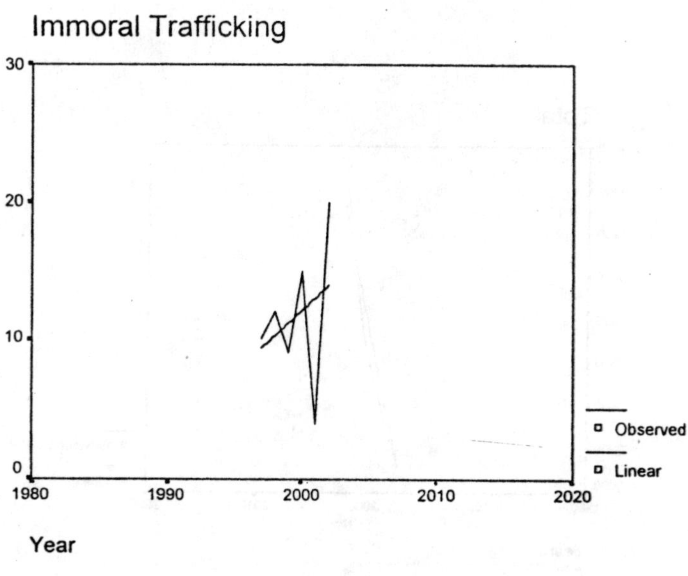
Immoral Trafficking
30
20
10
0
1980
1990
2000
2010
2020
Year
Observed
Linear

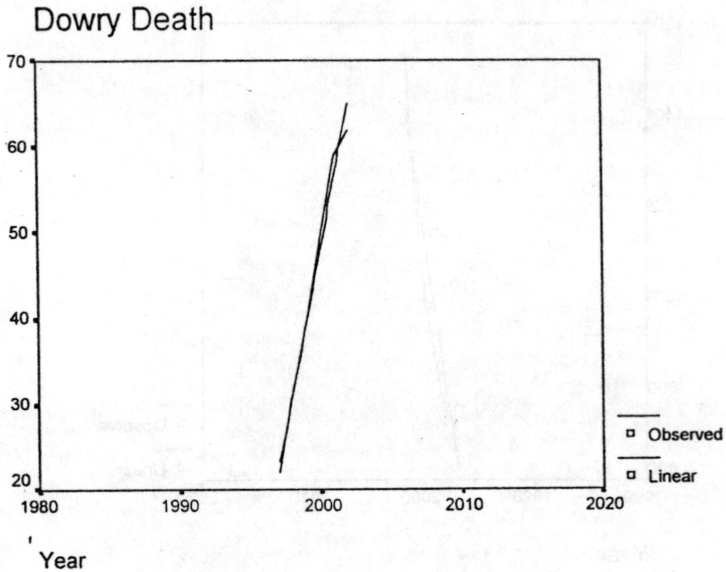
Dowry Death
70
60
50
40
30
20
1980
1990
2000
2010
2020
Year
Observed
Linear

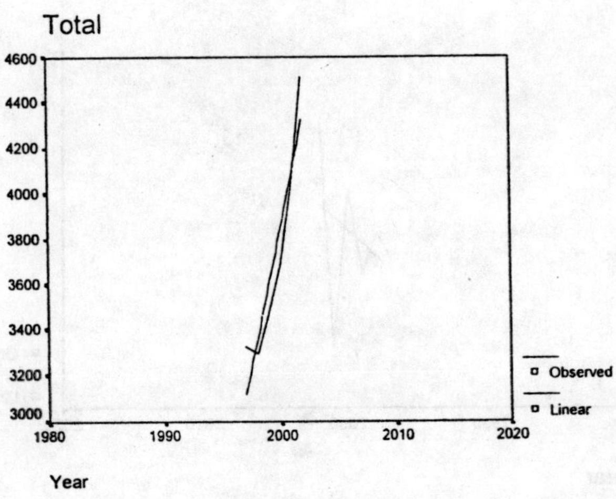
Total
4600
4400
4200
4000
3800
3600
3400
3200
3000
1980
1990
2000
2010
2020
Year
Observed
Linear

Inter District distribution of crime against women

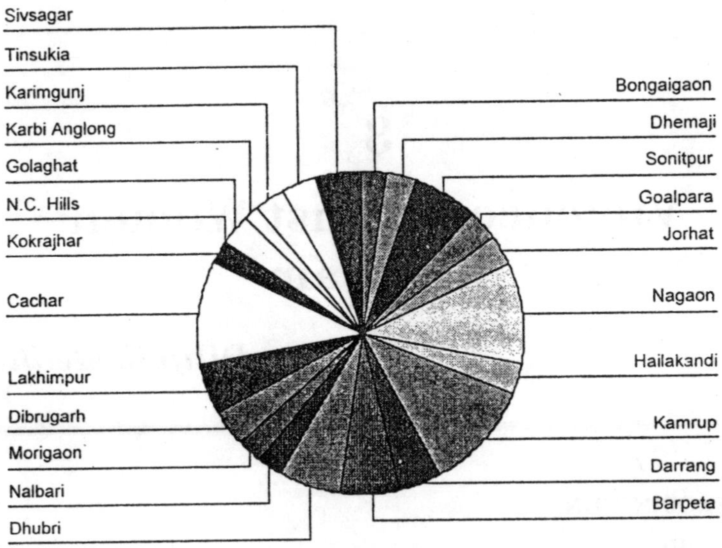

References

Ahuja R, 1998. *Violence against Women.* Jaipur: Rawat Publications.

Âmâr Axom, 8 April 2003.

Ibid., 9 June 2003.

Asomiyâ Pratidin, 16 July 2002.

The Hindu, Sept. 01, 2002.

Ibid., July 14, 2002.

Ibid., Aug 04, 2002.

Ibid., Oct 09, 2002.

Planning Commission of India. Volume II. *The Tenth Five-Year Plan, 2002-2007.* Government of India, New Delhi.

Sâdin, 29th November 2002.

Saxena, S., 1995.*Crimes against Women and Protective Laws*. New Delhi: Deep and Deep Publications.

Sinha, N, 1989. *Women and Violence.* New Delhi: Vikas Publishing House.

The Week, Feb 03, 2002

3

Violence Against Women in Assam

—*Dilip K. Medhi*

INTRODUCTION

Why does violence against women commonly occur in human society is a major question to the social scientists and also to the law enforcement departments all over the world. It has considerable significance to the so-called human civilization, civilized nationhood and of course to the entire human world. Violence against women is often referred to as 'inhuman' and 'brutal'.What is the primary factor that makes the humankind to commit crime against its feminine gender? Is it gender discrimination or simply does a male do it upon consideration of the physical powerlessness in female in general? These are some of the questions to be addressed in presentation of a write-up on violence against woman. Moreover the issue requires certain understanding on the part of the social scientists to make certain detailed analysis of the classificatory framework of different categories of crimes presented by the law enforcement agencies.

The writer is also concerned with the status of woman in this regard. Any violence against woman, the writer considers as a great molestation of the status of woman or rather against the great motherhood of humankind. In rural areas of Assam, the male folk often use slang abuses as a common address of abuse during a feud. They are mischievous and certainly go against the status of woman in the human World. It is much ridiculous but male never cares to refrain from such habit. The writer has plenty of personal experiences of folk abuse in and around his birthplace in Barpeta district of Assam.

National Crime Records Bureau, Ministry of Home Affairs, Government of India writes, "Global campaign for elimination of violence against women in recent years indicates the enormity as well as seriousness in the atrocities committed against women that are witnessed world over".

Media all over the world particularly the newspapers often gives considerable coverage on violence against women. Few years back a dalit woman was marched naked on the street in open daylight in a part of Northern India. In the month of November 2003, a girl was raped in the train in Bihar. Everyone is acquainted with the famous 'Tandoori murder case' of Delhi. This along with another case of murder of poetess Madhumita by a politician this year in Uttar Pradesh created substantial sensation all over India. In the early part of 2003, a girl eloped with her boy friend and she was later deserted by the latter and was subsequently raped by a group of youths at Guwahati. In another case of that period, a young married lady of Santipur, Guwahati could escape from the atrocities of her husband at dead hours of the night and now lives with her parents owing to insufficient amount of dowry. In another case in the same locality, a man burnt his wife to death, and lack of evidence enabled him to marry again. At Shrimantapur area of the city of Guwahati a woman was murdered for an exaggerated demand of dowry in 2002 after she was physically tortured every evening camouflaged by high volume of their TV set by the husband and his family members. In another case at Guwahati, a husband burnt his wife to death with kerosene oil in front of two kids. There are also evidences of rescuing young girls from Assam regions from different parts of mainland India, who were taken by some touts for the purpose of flesh trading. Further more, a Professor of Birubari had beaten his wife and they later began to live apart at the interference of their neighbours. Still other two cases are mentioned by the writer again in connection with the atrocities of husband and his relatives. Another Professor regularly ill-treated his wife in front of his sister and mother and later they got separated. The same Professor sexually harassed one of his lady colleagues and he was not punished although the victim (colleague) lodged a complaint to the authority. Another Professor sexually molested his student but was not punished due to indifferent attitude of the authority concerned. A former pilot of Air India regularly beats his wife on flimsy grounds and who also allegedly murdered his wife's elder brother who protested against such atrocities. It is true that a number of cases including many of them mentioned here go unreported due to interference of political and police machineries. Moreover many of the aboriginal communities in different parts of the world and in the Assam region as well resolve many criminal cases including those perpetrated on women in the framework of customary laws. Many families are reluctant to co-operate with any kind of enquiry that the police machinery wants to investigate. The current issue in this regard is aimed at discovering 'violence against women in the Assam region' and its nature and impact on the people of the area.

Under normal circumstances violence against women comprises,

1. Dowry death,
2. Ill treatment or torture by husband and his relatives,
3. Rape,
4. Kidnapping,
5. Sexual harassment,
6. Immoral trafficking of women,
7. Molestation and
8. Certain Undefined crimes.

Most of them are reported by Police department, and are common in Assam from time to time. Dowry related violence against women was never heard in this part of India as opposed to its occurrence in mainland India. But this type of violence begins to appear initially amongst the trading communities coming from mainland India, and now percolates to the local people in the recent past.

In recent years, Assam is experiencing a number of crimes against women and most particularly against young unmarried women. I personally know that on many occasions, visitors to the Gandhi Mandap at Saranaia Hills, Guwahati were sexually assaulted and many of them were not reported to the police on the ground that the victims belonged to some noted families of Guwahati. Husband's ill treatment or torture is of course much prevalent and reported from time to time. Cases of rape are increasing as reported by the media and the police departments. Kidnapping, particularly of minor girls is also occurring as a major concern of violence against women. In some parts of Upper Assam, young boys elope with young girls, marry them in some temples and afterwards desert them forever. In the past three years or more these kinds of cases are increasing in an alarming rate and have became a major criminal offence to the Assam police department as well the people in general, particularly the parents of the girls. Management bodies of some temples including the famous *Kamakshya* temple at Guwahati are taking preventive measure in this regard when their authorities inviting the parents of both the boys and the girls to authenticate their consents/permissions towards the proposed marriages. Travelling in a public transport and that too in a crowded city bus tells about some horrible experiences of young girls when they are molested in a calculated way by male passengers of any age. Molestation and eve teasing go together in such situations. Teasing a lady - both young and married on the street with all kinds of slang abuses is another way to perpetrate another kind of violence against women. Newspaper often reports about sexual harassment to teenager maidservants who become pregnant in the houses of their landlords. Further there are innumerable cases, which go unreported and never brought to the notice of the police department because of the standing of the victims and their families. In such cases, the police department becomes helpless in the investigation of such cases when neither the victim nor the family of the victim co-operates in the proceedings, and such cases become either settled or remained unsettled forever.

A murder occurred in the premises of 'Network Travel' in 2002. A teenager of around 9-years of age was first raped and then she was killed and her dead body was hidden in the septic tank of the Network Travel's premises, while she was sleeping with her parents. In another case a minor girl of around 4-years of age was raped by a shopkeeper. A boy friend killed his fiancé in the middle of the Brahmaputra River and threw away her body in the water. In another case, a boy friend murdered his fiancé in a hotel at Lakhtokia area of Guwahati and disposed of her body in a garbage bin of the city. In the year of 1975 at Barpeta, a young girl was murdered in cold blood by her boyfriend owing to her refusal to marry him. The first two cases are the clear evidence of sexual harassment on teenagers and the rest are all distinctively a kind of violence against woman. In early 2003, a lone elderly lady was killed in her residence by a group of dacoits at Kumarpara area of Guwahati in broad daylight and deserted with the property of her residence. In December 2003,another elderly lady of around 87-years age was similarly killed in her residence and the killers took away all the belongings of her household.

Starting from the Hindu religious mythology to the Oedipus complex, there are number of instances when status of women is abused with illicit relation and also with immoral atrocities and harassment. Lord Brahma married Lady Swarswati who was his own daughter by virtue of her creation. King Ravana kidnapped Lady Sita whom he later proposed to marry. Lord Rama punished Sita in an ordeal of fire (*agni-pariksha*) on a suspicion of Sita's chastity. Lady Draupadi was physically harassed in the open court of Hastinapur by Duryodhana and his brother Dusasana attempted to disrobe her. Oedipus complex is a crime related to sex taboo between sons and mother and rests of the cases those are referred to from Hindu mythology are also related to sex and molestation of status of women.

In the following tables (Table 3.1-3.3) and pie charts, a picture of the different categories of crime has been cited from year 1997 to 2000. The statistics reflects a level of all India crime rate with percentage against woman.

Table 3.1

Crime rate with percentage against women.

Category	Year			
	1997	1998	1999	2000
1. Torture	30.3%	31.5%	32.3%	32.4%
2. Dowry Death	5.8%	5.3%	4.9%	4.9%
3. Kidnapping & Abduction	12.8%	12%	11.7%	10.6%
4. Rape	12.6%	11.4%	11.4%	11.7%
5. Others	0.1%	0.2%	0.3%	0.5%
6. Sexual Harassment	4.8%	6.2%	6.5%	7.8%
7. Immoral Trafficking Prevention Act	6.9%	6.6%	6.9%	6.7%
8. Dowry Prohibition	2.2%	2.7%	2.2%	2.0%
9. Molestation	23.3%	23.4%	23.8%	23.3%

Sources : National Crime Record Bureau, Ministry of Home Affairs, New Delhi.

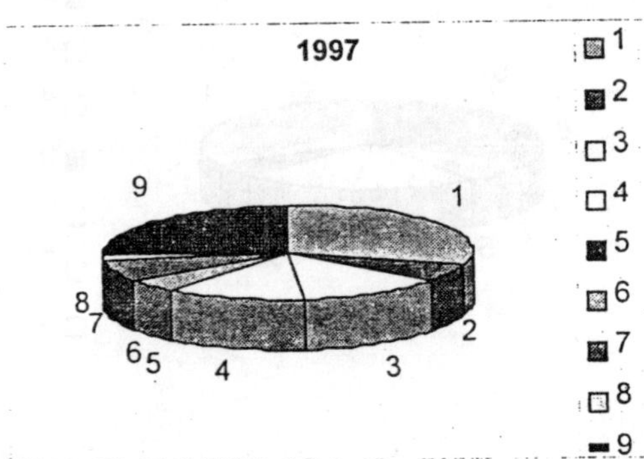

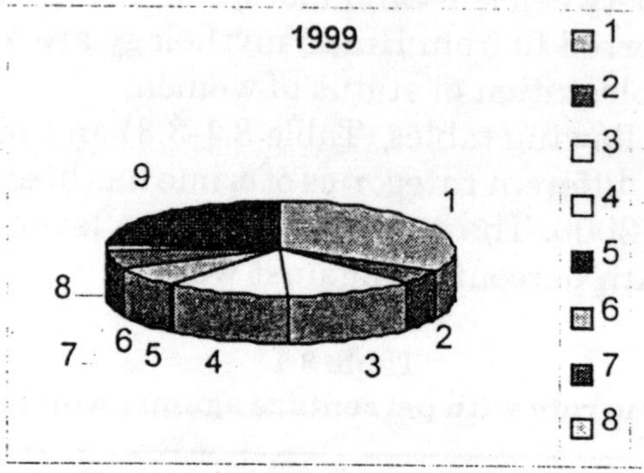

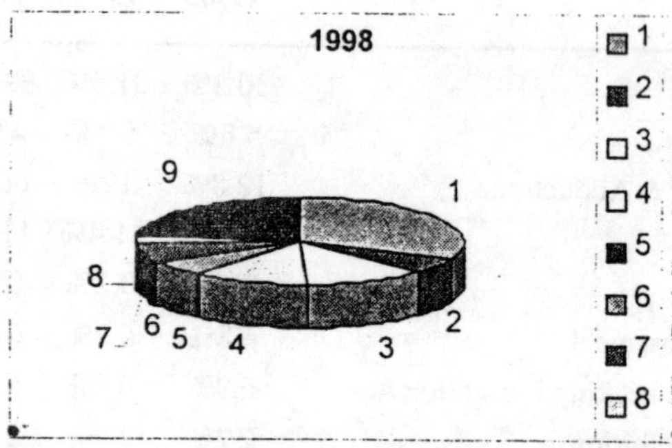

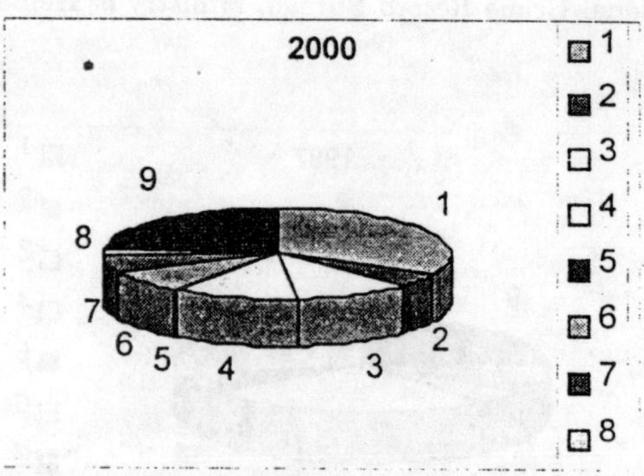

Sources: National Crime Record Bureau, Ministry of Home Affairs, New Delhi

Table 3.2

INCIDENCE AND RATE OF CRIMES AGAINST WOMEN IN INDIA

Year	Incidence of total crime	% Contribution of All India	Total (In Lakh)	Est. mid Yr. Population	Rank*	Rate of total Cogn. Crime Rank*
1997	3407	2.8	252.8	13.5	8	13
1998	3388	2.6	256.5	13.2	12	13
1999	3504	2.6	259.8	13.5	13	13
2000	3732	2.6	263.0	14.2	11	13

*Rank on the basis of total cognizable crime ** Rank on the basis of % share

Sources: National Crime Record Bureau. Ministry of Home Affairs, New Delhi.

Table 3

INCIDENCE AND RATE OF CRIMES AGAINST WOMEN IN THE STATE OF ASSAM

1	2	3			4			5		
		I	R	P	I	R	P	I	R	P
1997	252.8	717	2.8	4.7	1113	4.4	7.1	2.2	0.1	0.4
1998	256.5	744	2.9	4.9	1117	4.4	6.8	32	0.1	0.5
1999	259.8	703	2.7	4.9	1149	4.4	7.2	40	0.2	0.6
2000	263.0	762	2.9	4.6	1101	4.2	7.3	50	0.2	0.7

6			7			8			9			10		
I	R	P	I	R	P	I	R	P	I	R	P	I	R	P
775	3.1	2.1	686	2.7	2.2	34	0.1	0.6	0.0	0.0	0 0.0	0.0	0.0	0:0
739	2.9	1.8	648	2.5	2.1	12	0.0	0.1	0.0	0.0	0 0.0	0.0	0.0	0.0
843	3.2	1.9	720	2.8	2.2	21	0.1	0.2	0.0	0.0	0 0.0	0.0	0.0	0.0
978	3.7	2.1	777	3.0	2.4	18	0.1	0.2	0.0	0.0	0 0.0	0.0	0.0	0.0

1. Year
2. Estimated Mid Year Population
3. Rape
4. Kidnapping & Abduction
5. Dowry Death
6. Cruelty by husband & Relatives
7. Molestation
8. Sexual Harassment (Eve-teasing)
9. Importation of Girls
10. *Sati* Prevention

Sources: National Crime Record Bureau, Ministry of Home Affairs, New Delhi.

Analysis

In Northeast Indian states or the Assam region, crimes against woman in the name of 'Importation of Girls' and 'Sati' are not reported. Cruelty by husband and relatives of the husband is a commonly occurring atrocity on women. A distantly related niece of this writer told about her experience in bus travel in the city when she could discover that most of the time they were sexually harassed by elderly males. Atrocities on woman or violence against woman do reflect either a so-called authority of man on women or because of an inherent lack of defence on the part of the woman.

Conclusion

Crime against women in Assam is on a moderately increasing trend, police department says. But a considerable amount of awareness is maintained to contain violence against women since it is a worldwide phenomenon. Surprisingly some kinds of crime on young women occur in the city of Guwahati, which really perturb the police department. Violence against young women are increasing in Upper Assam and also at Guwahati, and, therefore the C.I.D. management of Assam Police is currently envisaged to take up a research project in this respect to get the actual cause of such happenings and in order to stop such crime in future.

4

Violence against Women in Manipur

—Esther Chinnu

Violence against women is a manifestation of the historically unequal power relations between men and women, which led to domination over and discrimination against women by men. The World Women's Conference, Beijing, 1995 shows the platform of action towards women's full advancement. Women, the world over, face violence due to the patriarchal structure present in the society. The reality and threat of violence is a hindrance in a woman's life and limits her ability to participate and contribute fully to the society. In the North East India, women enjoy greater mobility and visibility than women of other communities in the country. Also practices such as dowry and bride burning are not very prevalent in the region. The above, however, is often cited to portray a picture of equity between men and women in the region. This has also given rise to the presumption that violence against women is not a major issue of concern in the northeast region.

Violence against women can be of any form such as wife beating, marital rape, dowry related violence, sexual abuse, desertion, forced pregnancy, forced sterilization and abortion, coercive use of contraceptives, female infanticide, prenatal selection, sexual harassment and intimidation at work, in the educational institutions and elsewhere, trafficking in women and forced prostitution etc.

North East Network (NEN) is an organization that believes that women's collective action will bring about a societal change. It is committed to gender justice, changing perspectives of the women of the region from needs to rights and ensure the framing of gender just policies. NEN believes in the progress of society on peace both inside and outside the homes, creating a culture of peace by women's active and informed involvement and by enhancing women's leadership roles.

North East Network conducts research works, field surveys on any of the topics related to our work and also provides training, networks with different women's groups in the regional, national and international levels. NEN works directly in the states of Assam, Meghalaya, Nagaland, Mizoram and Manipur.

Data collected by North East Network (from field reports, inputs from monthly health collectives meetings, conferences, workshops and surveys which the organization has been conducting over the past couple of years), however, suggest that violence against women, particularly domestic violence, is on the rise in the region. It is a critical area of concern. Registered cases of crimes against women in Manipur reflect that instances of domestic violence are steadily increasing. It is important to note that more than half of the incidences of violence against women is never reported to any enforcement agency or to the authorities. Therefore data collected on such incidences are underreported and cannot represent the current situation of the state.

Violence against women has an impact on the health of women too. According to Dr. R. K. Lenin, Assistant Professor, Psychiatry Department, Regional Institute of Medical Sciences, Imphal, 'Mental health of women is lower than men. Mental problems are two times higher among women and only a fraction of it takes treatment. Ten per cent of the total population suffers from mental illness out of which 1% is very severe'. He elaborates to say that women go for treatment only in extreme cases when pathological problems manifest in the forms of severe headache, backache, depression or general ill- health. The study conducted by North East Network also showed that they lack of support systems to address the problems of mental health. Several NGOs have initiated efforts to help restoring the above issue. One such effort has been that of the North-East Network. With a view to build community level support services to address trauma being faced by women, North East Network has held an intensive training of trainers on Trauma Counselling (over three phases) for women's groups representing different communities (both tribal and non-tribal) in Manipur.

The breakdown of the formal health care services in certain areas due to the ongoing conflict is the other major area of concern. This has specially affected women, as they have to travel for several kilometres to meet their health needs. The ongoing-armed conflict situation and unrest prevalent in the Northeast has intensified the violence faced by women, which takes the forms of sexual, mental or physical abuses or killings and clashes. There have been ethnic conflicts between different groups in the state .The local aspirations and needs not being understood or paid heed to the region became a cauldron of conflict with demands and counter demands. The region has, thus, been witnessing to a low intensity war like situation for the past few decades. Although all members of communities are impacted in situations of armed conflict, it has special repercussions on the status of women. The impact on women and girls is far worse because of their status in society and their sex. The region has witnessed a resurgence of patriarchal values and norms which brought about along with new restrictions imposed on the movement of women, dress they wear and more overtly physical violence such as rape, which is systematically used as a tactic against a particular individual or community.

It is noteworthy that women in Manipur play a critical role in economy and trade in the state. Women also control large proportions of trade in the state in essential commodities. The market places are central to women's community life and organizing activities. Women of Manipur have their own spaces in the central market famously known as the IMA KEITHEL. The market women have led many of the mass movements, which characterize the history of the early part of the 20th century in Manipur. Women's hold over economy has been a major contributory factor in their ability to function as agents of change in society. However paradoxically, their economic contribution has not resulted in a corresponding position of influence in political participation and decision-making.

Despite the fact that there has been very strong women's activism in the state of Manipur starting from the early part of the century, the women in Manipur are the worst affected by the ongoing conflict. It has led to the increased instances of violence against women, wherein women are targeted both by state and non-state actors due to their status in society and their sex. Women have been victims of mental, physical and sexual violence in the whole process. It has been estimated that 3 to 4 rape cases occurring in situations of conflict go unreported .The myths attached to rape linked with concepts of 'chastity', 'morality' and 'family honour' and the code of silence maintained by the society leave the victim vulnerable to shame and social stigma. There have been instances where women who resisted rape by perverted *father-in-law*, *uncle- in-law* or *brother-in-law* were beaten and later deserted on some other grounds. Child sexual abuse is on the rise. Newspaper reports in Manipur have filled the daily columns of children being abused not only by strangers but also by trusted family members and relatives.

It has been reported that some jawans of the 6th Manipur Rifles posted at the complex of the Guwahati High Court, Imphal Bench tried to rape two minor girls after they were forcefully abducted from the gate of the court room number 2. The Imphal Free Press, English Daily reported on 15th March 2003 that a case has been registered at the Manipur Human Rights Commission on the basis of a petition filed by a house wife of Haorang Sabal regarding the rape of her minor daughter in February 2003 by a 22 year old youth. The Imphal Free Press also reported on 26th March 2003, that a man identified as Khwairakpam Gulamjit apparently disappointed over the birth of a baby girl tried to abandon the child after smuggling her out from the Gynaecology ward, Regional Institute of Medical Sciences, Imphal. Fortunately for the child and her mother the alert security personnel of the hospital came about upon the child near the isolated ward of the hospital and rescued her. The Sangai Express, on 26th Ferbruary 2003 reported that a PIL has been filed by a group of NGOs in connection with raping of one Meinam Bina Devi of Luwangshangbam Matai Mamang Leikai by personnel of 25 Assam Rifles on October 6th 2001. The Zalen Banner (a kuki newspaper) reported on 13th August 2002 that a 7 year old girl had been raped by K. Ibocha Singh, 51 years at Moirang Pansang, Bishnupur District of Manipur. The Sangai Express reported on 20th February 2003 that Laimayum Ram Sharma, Commmunication Officer, Regional Health and Family Welfare Training Center, Porompat tried to sexually molest her daughter in-law on November 14 the earlier year and has been suspended from 23rd November.The source also mentioned that Ram's wife Binodini Devi, who admitted taking her son into confidence and instigated the victim girl to undergo abortion twice so that she would remain childless was arrested following a complain filed by the victim. Binodini also confessed the charges of ill-treating her daughter-in-law and not even allowing her to cook meals or to touch water of the family as she belongs to lower middle/lower caste. Husband of the victim Laimayum Rakesh Sharma who had eloped with another girl namely K.Reena Devi has been absconding.

The Sangai Express reported on the 30th March 2003 about the gruesome murder of Mayanglambam Sumatibala of Tera Tongbram Leikai on December 15th 2002 by Kiran who revealed that he had fallen in love with the deceased and had been having illicit relation since some years back and on the virtue of it, she pursued him to marry her at the earliest,it said. Kiran being already married kept on postponing and the girl had asked him to compensate her financially; unable to cope with the pressure Kiran killed her. The Sangai Express reported on 29th October 2002 about the rape of a mentally challenged girl of 14 years by unknown culprits who caught her and repeatedly raped her. A cloth was stuffed inside the mouth of the victim to silence her cries of protest. The Sangai Express reported on 16th July 2002 about the rape of a social worker by one Pheiroijam Babu Singh, PSO to a political leader in the house of one policeman at Utlou Makha Leikai. The victim also reported that three other police personal and three civilians assisted the PSO in raping her. The Imphal Free Press reported on 14th January 2003 that a woman identified as Mayanlambam Sobhapati Devi, 20, of Urup Arapti Makha Leikai under Singjamei police station, Imphal narrowly escaped death when she was hacked by her husband. According to reports, Manihar, 35 years of age, son of Yamjou committed suicide after attacking his wife. The Imphal Free Press reported on 5th July 2002 about the forced abortion done on a young unmarried girl by her boyfriend and his mother in order to avoid marrying the girl. The foetus was two months old.

Manipur does not have a State Commission for Women to handle crimes against women and to lend a voice to the women in the state. The Manipur Human Rights Commission (MHRC) constituted on 27th June 1998 is a state institution, which has been handling cases of violations of Human rights. As on August 2002, 648 cases pertaining to Human Rights abuse had been registered with MHRC. (*The Telegraph*, 28th August 2002).

Table 4.1
THE NUMBER OF RAPE CASES REGISTERED WITH THE MHRC

Year	Number of cases
2000	15
2001	8
2002	5.(till July)

Source: Resource Directory North East Network Manipur. 2003.

Table 4.2
STATISTICS ON CRIME AGAINST WOMEN, 1999-2000 (UP TO AUGUST)

Crime Head	No. of cases reported during the year			
	1999	2000	2001	2002 (Up to Aug)
1. Murder	11	11	2	2
2. Rape	10	12	16	7
3. Molestation	14	29	36	24
4. Kidnapping	42	40	69	56
5. Assualt	12	9	12	29
6. Suicide	8	11	4	-
7. Women Burning	-	-	-	1
8. Others	8	7	8	15
Total	105	119	147	134

Source: Resource Directory North East Network Manipur. 2003.

Table 4.3

THE TOTAL NUMBER OF CASES FILED AT FAMILY COUNSELLING CENTRE, JULY 1998 TO DECEMBER 2001

1.	Maintenance Demand Case	137
2.	Cruelty by in-laws	36
3.	Desertation	45
4.	Claiming of Dowry Goods after separation	5
5.	Drug related problems	12
6.	Disputes of Family/old age pension	20
7.	Destitute Women /Children	7
8.	Bride Price Demand	2
9.	Child Custody	19
10.	Extended help to 23 families below poverty line	
11.	Property dispute	49
12.	Family Maladjustment	64
13.	Marital	19
14.	Divorced Cases	15
15.	Handicapped & Mentally retarded cases	4
16.	Illegal Separation	3
17.	Inter-Caste Marriage	3
18.	Juvenile Delinquent Cases	4
	Total	**737**

Source : Resource Directory North East Network Manipur, 2003.

Domestic violence is another area of concern. Registered cases of crimes against women in Manipur reflect that instances of domestic violence are steadily increasing. Women's health is severely affected.

Regarding the health of women, the rising instances of HIV/AIDS and its impact on woman is an area of concern in the state. Our work in the field level shows that although both men and women with HIV/AIDS are discriminated against, the level of discrimination and violence faced by women is much higher. We came across a number of cases wherein the husband infected the wife, but as soon as the woman was detected with HIV/AIDS, she was thrown out of the house. In other case, woman was expected to care for her husband, but after his death, she was not allowed to stay in the same house by *her-in-laws*. In almost all the cases women were blamed for being the carrier of the virus. Women with HIV/AIDS were often denied access to nutritious food and often had to go without food. Their family and friends regard women and men with HIV/AIDS as outcasts. Even the church most often takes a moralistic view of the whole issue. Thus, it is very difficult for women to come out and seek help. Death due to HIV/AIDS infection in Churachandpur district till March 2002 unofficially is 400 according to Dr. Muana, Director, Shalom (Society for HIV/AIDS and Lifeline Operation in MANIPUR).

Armed conflict has given rise to many women headed households. For several women, this meant they being forced to access to the formal economic sector to earn means of livelihood for the first time. In the course of our fieldwork, we found that often women have to resort to selling liquor, drugs or even go into prostitution to make enough money to run their households. Again, when men are killed during conflict, the families hardly get the ex-gratia. Even if, it is mostly the boy's parents who determine who will benefit from it. In this process, the wife of the person usually loses out.

Ethnic clashes in Manipur have resulted in mass scale displacement of families. Many of these families are settled in relief camps. Basic infrastructural facilities like food, safe drinking water and medicines are lacking in these camps. In makeshift provisions it is usually women who have to sustain their families by gathering firewood, ensuring food security, clothing etc. They ensure that their children, elderly members and husbands survive.

Apart from the direct impact of the conflict in terms of violence, loss of property and livelihoods, displacement and trauma, patriarchal controls on women seem to have increased. Women are expected to be the torchbearers of the culture and traditions but are excluded from decision-making bodies. Even in human rights organizations and peace initiatives women do not play a decisive role.

The Meira Paibis are among the most known women's movement in Manipur. Among the Meiteis, the Meira Paibis have roamed the streets and locality to keep watch on alcohol and drug abuses. The first night patrol was organized in 1975. By 1976, the movement had spread and night patrolling was a regular sight in Imphal .The night patrollers started to bring down drinking habits amongst the men in Manipuri society so as to prevent alcoholism from affecting 'normal' family life and encourage men's participation in productive activities. In the recent years the Meira Paibis have been involved in humanitarian activities in Manipur especially working on issues relating to atrocities by the state and the armed forces. They are the only sections of people who have accessed and to some extent moral authority over insurgents. Many women who are part of the Meira Paibis have been lathi charged. They sit for hunger strikes and have been jailed for causes they believe in. In the 1990's when extension of Armed Forces Special Powers Act transformed Manipur into a garrisoned state, women were in the forefront of the struggle against human rights violations by the security forces. Other than the Meira Paibis, women from almost all communities have been organized and have been part of various movements.

Tangkhul Shanoa Long (TSL) has been particularly active in trying to minimize the traumatic impact of violence in the community. In July 1997 following an ambush by the NSCN-IM, the Assam Rifles, a central para-military force, went on a rampage in Ukhrul town. There was a great sense of terror in the region. It was in this situation that the TSL initiated a dialogue with the army and persuaded them to release civilians. In an effort to instil confidence in the townspeople and the adjoining villages, they appealed to the shopkeepers to open their shops and encouraged the people who had fled their homes to return. They forced the village elders to bring peace in Churachandpur district to stop Naga-Kuki killings in 1995.

The Kuki Women's Union together with the Naga Women's Union of Manipur has played a crucial role during the Naga- Kuki clashes, where barbarism got unleashed in the name of ethnic cleansing. Manipuri women groups have literally been the watch dogs of their society. For example, in the Bizang Community Camp which was established after ethnic clashes between Kuki and Zomi in Churachandpur District, the Zomi Mothers Association, and, Kuki Women's Union have been working for the people of both sides. They have distributed clothes and food during the conflicts. Women have played an important role in trying to get these communities together. An orphanage has been established by the Kuki Women's Union called Sanga Muon Inn for the children whose parents have been killed in the conflict.

The Naga Women's Association (NMA) though based in Nagaland, has collaborated with women on Naga areas in Manipur. The agenda has been to bring peace amongst all groups. NMA launched its campaign 'shed no more blood' in which they called for a halt to all kinds of killings. They initiated a dialogue with the state and the underground for a ceasefire. NMA has also been instrumental in securing a promise from NSCN-K group not to retaliate when tensions arose in times of killings and murders. One of the pamphlets displays the following message: 'The assassinated man may be a husband, a father, a son or a brother'.

In keeping with old traditions the Naga Women Union of Manipur (NWUM), together with members of the Naga Mother's Association of Nagaland have started the process of bringing about reconciliation between the different Naga rival militant groups with a view to put an end to the ethnic and factional killings. The attempt has not been easy with women having to undertake long arduous journeys on foot to meet leaders and appeal to put an end to killings. In addition, they have been extremely vulnerable to suspicion and security risks. This took place in March 2000 and recently in 2002.

Having said this, the status of women in Manipur needs analysis because certain aspects of their lives may not seem entirely empowering. For one, high level of participation in a movement does not necessarily mean equal decision making powers at all levels. Among the tribal communities in the region, one major hurdle is the non-participation of women in the decision- making process. This is a much revered customary norm and practice. While local legal and quasi legal practices in most parts of India got assimilated in the judicial system of the British India, tribal communities of the North East India were by and large left free to be regulated by their own conception of law and by their own machinery .The policy of non- interference has contributed positively towards preserving the customs, traditions, ways of life and cultural patterns of the communities. But our customary laws prevent women from making decisions. Although there are several provisions of the customary laws, which promote gender equity and ensure that rights are maintained yet, not all-customary laws are gender sensitive. Some examples of the above are:

In most tribes, including the Kukis, if a woman does not have a son, inheritance is near impossible. In such cases, after the death of the husband, custody of the children as well as property rights are automatically with *herin-laws.*

Women have no inheritance rights, and even if a father may leave properties in his daughter's name, the male cousins of the girl will claim them after the death of the father.There is a need for a movement to emerge within communities to bring about a change in the customary laws and to ensure that the rights of all laws need to be codified, reinvented in accordance with the present situation.

The second aspect of women's low status is seen in the earlier practice of polygamy. This was adopted by coincidence rather than by design where the loss of men in the Manipuri-Burmese war was significantly high. The unequivocal need for social security gave way to elders sanctioning polygamy as a means of security and protection to women. This has, however, become a practice among the Meitei community and is extremely discriminatory towards women. The third aspect is that of the sanskritisation process that had a significant impact on the Meitei society, which at present is largely hinduised. Present day norms followed in Meitei Society are rather strict for women in the household.

An organization like the North East Network (NEN) has been consistently working at addressing the structural causes of violence against women and to question and examine gender inequalities. Although women in Manipur are relatively better than those in other parts of the country, yet to achieve equality a basic change in the power structure is required. It is also important that the state recognizes the need of addressing the issue and comes forward with positive support.

5

Alcohol and Drug-Related Violence against Women in Manipur

—Salam Irene

To effectively address the issue of violence against women (VAW) one needs to build an understanding of the structural causes of violence, and also to take into account the gender dimensions of the same. Young women are especially vulnerable to coerced sex and rape. Many such women are under the age of twenty. Short changing girls is not only a matter of gender discrimination, it is bad economics and bad social policy[1]. But women suffer violence all throughout their life cycle. Census figures, 2001 show that there are 933 Indian women for every 1000 men. So, where are the missing girls? Gender-based violence and exploitation continues unabated. Most girls' sexual encounters are coercive and violent, especially when the partners are under the influence of drugs/alcohol. Estimates place the number of Indian girls sold to brothels at 5000-7000 annually. The practice has been extended beyond national borders. Simultaneously, the number of girls and young women affected and infected by HIV/AIDS is increasing[2]. Women's low economic and social status leaves them vulnerable to unwanted sexual activity and negates access to accurate and adolescent friendly reproductive health information. More than 6 million of the estimated 10.3 million young people infected with HIV/AIDS are girls. In Manipur, there is a definite co-relation between injecting drug use (IDU) and rapid transmission of HIV to IDUs partners and children. The AIDS pandemic in Manipur has assumed a new dimension with a large section of people in the productive age group, 21- 30, beginning to fall prey to the disease. The number of HIV positive pregnant women is on the rise viz., 2.4% in March 2003[3]. Of the 14,937 blood samples tested positive in Manipur, 2,178 samples are of women.

In one of its editorials in a local daily paper, The Imphal Free Press, it had correctly reported that one of the factors that is throwing the state into total atrophy is the fact that increasingly the idea of violence as a language is being given legitimacy precisely by lack of credible and effective governance. There is a general failure to recognize the systematic nature of women's subordination. There is a tendency to view abuse and violation of women's human rights as individual aberrations rather than as gender-based violence. The reluctance to characterize the subordination of women as human rights violation is a result of deep-rooted cultural, traditional and age-old practices. Even the state, which is generally ready to regulate and intrude into most areas of civil life especially with regard to freedom of expression, is singularly averse to interfering in the private area of family.

Key issues which women's groups in India identified during the Beijing process included the need for transformative education, reproductive rights, freedom from violence and women's human rights. In totality, the UN Beijing Conference in 1995 identified a substantial agenda of actions needed to enable women to enjoy full human rights, to have access to critical resources like land and water and to realize their potential contribution to national development. It is now well documented that more enlightened gender policies and investments in women's education and health lead to higher human development and economic growth. But, while human rights violations occur largely in the public sphere and are perceived as perpetuated and redressed by the state, the private sphere is inferior to the public sphere. And it is in the private sphere that most alcohol and drug related violence against women occurs.

The average age at which Indian men develop alcohol dependence today is 29 years. Forty four per cent of middle level executives stress for their higher level of alcohol consumption. Despite prohibition being in force in Manipur for more than a decade and drug use being recognized as public health emergency (in 1995), alcohol and drug use is common among all sections and strata of society. Use of liquor is also customarily related with traditional rituals and festivities, especially in the hill areas of the state (home brewed rice liquor). Practically in every village liquor is brewed according to the requirements of its populace.

Women are especially vulnerable to alcohol and drug related violence. There is a definite link between increase in alcohol intake and increase in wife and child abuse. Any individual under the influence of alcohol loses his inhibitions and in an inebriated state doesn't think twice about inflicting insults, humiliations viz., verbal, physical, psychological, emotional upon family members who are usually already asleep or partly asleep when the intoxicated family member returns home in the late evening or night. And intoxicated individuals have a habit of raising their voices, repeating the same phrases/sentences over and over again until they are successful at provoking or goading other family members especially wives into an argument/quarrel. The breath and body odour of alcoholics is generally nauseating and unpleasant to women and children, a source of humiliation and embarrassment before members of the extended family/ locality. Very often the alcoholic is unsteady on his feet and falls down flat on his face ignomously. The alcoholic's irresponsible behaviour becomes public knowledge. Women and children in the family become timid, subservient, afraid and emotions are born out of sense of shame.

A survey of an International Institution of Population Studies revealed attitudes that justify, if not condone wife beating. Women are not just beaten, but psychologically, sexually and emotionally abused. As a part of alcohol related violence, male drug users are not as a rule physically violent, instead they have recourse to manipulation in which they possess great proficiency and often forcing their partners into coerced sex, which results not only in the spread of communicable diseases like STD's and HIV, but also in unwanted or early pregnancy, unsafe abortion, early unplanned marriage. Early marriages before women have developed sense of autonomy result in unequal relations between women and men rendering women more vulnerable to VAW.

The International Centre for Research on Women estimates that 60% of women face violence at some point in their marriage. What is abuse? A woman is often easy prey to abuse within her relationships. Physically and financially weaker, she takes on the role of the less aggressive partner. Wrapping her identity around her marriage, she holds on to this fragile sense of security for life. When children step in, the woman makes more space for them and less even emotionally for herself. In her new role as a tigress protecting her cubs, she is more willing to maintain the harmony in her home[4]. Usually, women affected by alcoholic abuse assume this mantle of tigress. Most women urban/rural for years bear alcoholism and abuse silently and they are unable to stand up against their own husbands. But in a specific act of abuse, can good women collectively act in defence of their interests Whimpering wives stoically bearing out beatings and humiliation, can turn the table over, and beat their own menfolk - a humiliation, no man wants to undergo. Some women are prodded into action because of the fear that their grown-up sons may take to drinking like their fathers[5].

Manipur is a state with a society in transition in which traditional social support systems have given way to the emergence of nuclear families, where both working parents have inadequate time generally to inculcate/reinforce sound moral values in their offspring. However, it is in their teen years that adolescents needed to be provided proper guidance, so as to cope with the changes taking place in the bodies at puberty. Young women including teenage girls are simultaneously the fastest growing risk group with regard to HIV/AIDS because of their generally lower status, inadequate empowerment with reference to decision-making and social norms of acceptable behaviour, which have been handed down over centuries. They lack access to preventive interventions and technologies, treatment, care and support. A general lower quality of health of many Indian women also increases their vulnerability to infection, thus becoming a major factor in the spread of the epidemic[6].

This is even more pertinent to women suffering from STI's.Where violence is seen as a means of monitoring and correcting women's behaviour, women may be as likely as men, to believe that it is appropriate to beat a women for certain transgressions, including covert contraceptive use. But most young women have inadequate knowledge/ information on reproductive health and rights and are easily manipulated through control over their sexuality and fertility. Even for women who possess this knowledge, there is a constant contradiction between the need and desires of the individual and the demand of society. Moreover, no other area is as potentially risky when involving men than counseling and testing for STI's especially HIV. Women are justifiably fearful of partner violence or abandonment if they are found to have an STI or be sero-positive.

This should not blind us to the fact that the historic focus on services for women has led to neglect of men's need for reproductive health information and services, often to the disadvantage of both women and men. Men are often less knowledgeable about anatomy and physiology than women, but more reluctant than women to show their ignorance. Often, as a result of this ignorance, young men in college and even teenage boys in schools get their girlfriends pregnant. A survey in India documented that even educated men lack knowledge about reproductive issues. But taking advantage of a young women's naivetee and innocence to coerce her into a physical relationship, is a form of VAW practiced on young women especially by intoxicated men, on a 'high' from drugs/alcohol, or both together. Although while intoxicated, these men are resistant/oblivious to the concept of gender equity, fearing to lose power/manliness, to which they feel entitled, there is an urgent need to promote change in gender dynamics. It is also important to look at young women separately, especially high school and college students, as their knowledge and attitudes are likely to be different from that of older women, as also their sources or lack of sources of information. They generally have limited access to information, and smaller social networks, more so, in the hill areas of Manipur.

The use of mind-altering substances goes back to the historical records we have from several early cultures and civilizations. The first sanskrit texts of ancient Indian civilization, the hymns and the poems of the Vedas describe the use of a still-mysterious agents, soma, which some scholars regarded as being hallucinogenic mushrooms and others, as more likely to have been either an opiate or marijuana derivative. Marijuana itself is described in the Ayurveda as usefu. for poets, musicians, singers, saints and manual labourers. A review of history suggests that in many cultures and times, mind-altering agents were not only a part of public life but a significant component of religious and ritual life.

Neither alcohol nor drug use is a recent phenomena in Imphal. Opium and ganja were used from the early times. But few people use these substances today, although the cultivation of ganja is still continuing both in the valley and hill districts of Manipur. Alcohol use is associated from early times with many rituals and festivities especially in the hill areas. But to understand the morphology of drug use, we need to refer to the history of opium, the parent agent of all opiate narcotics, including heroin, the drug of choice in Manipur. At the start of the last millennium it was arguably the most effective agent mankind had. While the opiates had many medicinal uses, they have probably always been addictive. The historical spread of poppy cultivation into South East Asia can only be guessed at, but by the time European explorers penetrated mainland South-East Asia from the 1600's onwards, opium was known and was used for its medicinal values. The most significant change in the history of opiate use came about in the late 18th/19th centuries, and involved interestingly financial issues raised by another psychoactive agent - tea. Both the British and the Dutch East India Companies were involved in the lucrative tea trade, then China's major agricultural export. Tea became more than popular in Europe and the demand for tea was immense but Ching dynasty, China had little demand for British goods. China wanted to trade tea for European and British silver. The result was a rapidly growing trade imbalance. Desperate to address the trade imbalance, and to find a product of interest to Chinese consumers, the British began importing increasing quantities of opium to China from Bengal then a British Indian colony.

For China, the results were devastating. Opium imports led to what may be one of the world's first and best-documented epidemics of opiate addiction. China banned opium trafficking but failed to control it. In 1840, China responded to this crisis with the farmers dumping of 20,000 chests of British opium into the South China sea. The victory of the British in the first opium war and the European victory in the Second Opium War, the dramatic expansion of poppy cultivation in Colonial India and the fortunes made in controlling the shipping and distribution of opium into China, the first great narcotics economy was born. As in China, colonial economic forces (French) created in Laos another narcotic based economy. While these historical events are well-documented, they are little understood or noted in today's debate on drug use. Two further interventions were to change the history of opiate use the syringe and heroin. Opium is not an ideal agent for injection but in the 1930's, morphine was methylated. Adding fat-soluble methyl groups made the new compound heroin and able to enter the brain much more quickly and efficiently. Through the 1930s and 1940s heroin, a pain agent, increasingly left the hospital and moved to the streets.

After the World War II, with the collapse of colonial empires and the emergence of Communist China, the opium industry in Asia went through profound changes. The defeated remnants of the Chinese National Army, the Kuo-Min-tang, who did not make it to Taiwan, fled into the hills of Northern Burma and began to develop the Shan, the Kokangand Wa regions, now so dominant in Asia's heroin trade. The Vietnam War era brought the Asia trade a gain into world focus. Burma, after General Win's coup, partnered with the KMT to supply the growing heroin demand among the United States forces in Indo-China. The next great change in opium came with the Soviet invasion of Afghanistan; the Afghan resistance, desperate for funds to buy munitions, turned to poppy cultivation and using opium to fund their war effort.

There is no accurate data about when the use of opiate and pharmaceutical drugs started in Manipur. Use of drugs like Prodrom, Mandrax, Calmpose etc. among the youth started in the early 1970's. Towards the end of 1970's, there was a transition towards injecting of morphine, norphine and pethidine. In the early 1980's, there was a scarcity of morphine in Imphal and the morphine injectors started using heroin as a substitute. Injecting of heroin is more economical than smoking or chasing it[7].

The Indo-Myanmar border of 1643 kms touches four states of the North East including Manipur (398 Km) . The terrain along the border belt is densely forested. The border is almost open. There are numerous jungle routes across the border, which are being utilized by smugglers, drug traffickers and other trans-border criminals without fear of detection by the security forces or the enforcement agencies. The population along the Indo-Myanmar border is tribal and almost all tribes have trans border ethnic contiguity. Mutually the residents are economically dependent and are in constant touch. Hill tribals inhabiting the border areas in India and Myanmar have traditionally enjoyed the facility of free movement up to 40 km either side of the border. The long and porous nature of the Indo-Myanmar border and the facility of movement without travel documents have led to the growth of smuggling activities on this border. Contraband goods enter India concealed in permissible head loads carried by the tribals. Many tribals viz., Nagas, Paites, Kukis, Lushais, Hmars etc. are inhabitants on both sides of the border. Identification or detection of illegal entrants is very difficult. Moreover, there is a substantial production of opium in Myanmar[8].

To decrease/ eliminate drug related violence against women, the reasons for drug use need to be understood. Drugs are easily available in many parts of the Northeast India and different vested interests continue to ensure their entry and distribution. Reasons for drug use are many - peer pressure, curiosity, lack of fear in experimenting with drugs, unemployment, lack of opportunities, disappointments and frustrations at home or outside the home, defiance, rebellion, lack of or no communication within a family (especially nuclear families), low self-esteem, poor decision-making skills, lack of social skills, lack of impulse control etc. Moreover the environment of Manipur characterized by a failing/bankrupt economy, lack of law and order, corruption in every sphere, have exacerbated the problem. Young people have nothing to look forward and are vulnerable to drug use and abuse. This tendency gets a further impetus from causative factors like relationship difficulties, illness, financial problems, academic failure, depression, poor mental health etc[9].

VAW is escalating to the extent that it is becoming a commonplace occurrence. Incidents of VAW are regularly reported in the local dailies. Although society and individuals do not dispute the fact that perpetrators of violence should be brought to book, such is the lacunae in our judicial system that very few culprits are actually punished and generally they are free to strike again with impunity. It is equally difficult for a woman victim of violence to file an FIR with the police. In order to curtail and gradually eliminate VAW, we must all analyze its causes.

Young men, especially adolescents in their late teens are sensitive, vulnerable, secretive, impatient, and defiant, yet possessed of a dynamic energy. This energy has to be channellised correctly and creatively so that disappointments resulting from a quarrel or rejection by a girlfriend, parents' refusal to purchase sundry articles demanded and deemed necessary by young men e.g., a motorcycle, car etc. Restrictions on mobility for example do not result in these young men/adolescent boys, finding solace in 'chasing the dragon, injecting illicit/licit drugs, drinking unrestrained quantities of alcohol. Such practices are regarded among peer groups as a form of deep bonding; deviations and non-participation being frowned upon. Under the influence of drugs/alcohol, many young men dating young women at 'Restaurants' in and around Imphal especially where seating arrangements place the couple in a compromising position, place these women at risk, as drugs and alcohol induce a state of euphoria where inhibitions have no place, and risky behaviour is the norm.

Young men and adolescent boys are unable to discuss their hopes, fears, ambitions, desires, sexual drive, insecurities with their parents/family members/community elders, they are also wary, hostile, unreceptive to advice/reprimand, and because of the traditional taboos on discussions on sexuality. There is an unmet need for counseling services so as to enable them to make an informed choice, while at the same time, respecting women's rights and choices. It is important to give young men a sense of self-worth so that they can define themselves, instead of letting others define them. However, women deserve special consideration from a biological, social and economic standpoint, especially when their health is at risk, by limiting their ability to use birth control without the partner's permission. The anti-retroviral drug nevirapine is administered free of cost to HIV infected pregnant mothers at JN Hospital, Imphal, to prevent parent -child transmission of HIV. Most women are infected through sexual transmission of the virus usually through no fault of their own (most women have only one life partner, who they believe to be mutually faithful). Although Nevirapine prevents parent-child transmission, after the birth of the baby, the infected mother finds it near impossible to access antiretroviral for herself because of the high cost of the regimen, and because of the discrimination, stigma, taboos associated with the disease. Despite the state-wide, mass awareness campaign on 'safe sex', it is important to remember that such emphasis with little understanding of the context in which safety is provided, is meaningless, for sexual and reproductive decisions are made against a backdrop of personal values, desires, morals, apprehensions, relationship and social pressures. The reality of women's lives is that they lack the power to say 'no' to unsafe sexual practices. Few young women have the opportunity/freedom to discuss issues of sexuality, desire, confusion, passion, doubt - they are instead socialized to be submissive and reticent, which leaves them unable to refuse sex or insist on safe sex with male drug and alcohol users. More and more young people are jeopardizing their lives, by smoking, ingesting, injecting drugs and drinking alcohol. It is a reality however, that drugs and alcohol have an appeal for young people at a susceptible time in their lives. Many young women, especially college students between the age of 17-25, have contracted STD's from their boyfriends or through promiscuous behaviour. According to an article in a popular daily, these infections are contracted at 'licentious parties' in the cities, mushrooming restaurants where drugs/alcohol are freely available (despite the ban on its use) and parties turn into sexual orgies, where the chances of girls (young women) becoming infected with STD, HIV, AIDS is very high, because of low or no condom use, and multiple sexual pairings[10]. Despite great strides in research and treatment in the field of medicine, nobody knows for sure, how long patients on new antiretroviral regimens will survive, before the virus finally out mutates the current armamentarium.

When teenagers begin to distance themselves from parents and family, the latter have to persist and ensure that lines of communication between them remain open. This is usually a disheartening and ungratifying exercise, but parents, despite sullen, provocative, aggressive, defiant behaviour of their offspring, must continue to support and demonstrate affection for their offspring during these crucial changing and turbulent years. This is of paramount importance especially in nuclear families, where parents provide the only support system. Changes in values, faster pace of life, competition, rivalry, and jealousy - all contribute in making young women sexually active much earlier than their peers, just a decade or two ago. Such young women are often physically attracted to male drug users, who in the prime of their youth are physically attractive, charming, and adept at manipulating emotions; as that proficiency/ability has already been finely honed to source money from parents, friends, girlfriends to buy their daily 'fix'.

To minimize VAW, raise greater awareness on the issue, mothers and daughters could come together to evolve practical strategies in 'ma-beti' (mother-daughter) melas, where through focused group discussions, women not only become aware of their rights, but know how to ensure that these rights are not infringed upon, either in private or public spaces e.g., how to fend off an unwelcome advance from an intoxicated person while commuting for work in public transport buses. Women must all possess management and livelihood skills, because economic independence is a vital tool for women's empowerment; women also need to acquire skills in networking, so that a victim of violence can easily and promptly access support mechanisms. As women work long hours, both in the house and outside, they are vulnerable not just to communicable diseases, but because of their 'double burden', to anaemia, physical and emotional stress, gynaecological problems etc. That is why, knowledge of reproductive health and rights should be about helping women and adolescents regulating their fertility safely and effectively, to conceive only if they so desire, and when they desire.

The responsibility of states for acts, which impair the rights of women, is sometimes mistakenly perceived as applying only when state agents or officials are the actual perpetrators of acts, which violate human rights. The protection afforded by human rights law is far greater. There is a clear responsibility on states under international law, which extends beyond violations by those acting on behalf of the state and its organs. The declaration on the elimination of violence, against women, adopted by the UN General Assembly in 1993 affirms that states must "Exercise due diligence to present, investigate and in accordance with national legislation, punish Acts of violence against women, whether those Acts are perpetrated by the state or by private persons"[11].

Applying international human rights law without understanding the responsibility of the state for abuses of women's rights by private actors including employers, partners, husbands, family members or neighbours - simply robs women of protection and of remedies for the majority of abuses against them.

The Indian Constitution upholds the right to equality before law (Article 14), and prohibits discrimination on the grounds of religion, race, caste, sex, or place of birth. Various laws reinforce safeguards against discrimination, and provide for positive discrimination for certain groups identified as vulnerable within society. These include scheduled castes and scheduled tribes and women.

On a more positive note 'recognizing its international commitments towards the rights of women and urge on by a dynamic women's movement, successive governments (in India) have unveiled policies of empowerment for women which have sought to address the full range of woman's human rights. The department of Women and Child Development began work on a national policy on women, which would seek to bridge the gap between the equal de-jure status and unequal de facto position of women in the country. The reality of the situation on the ground for women, however, continues to be extremely harsh despite the constitutional, legislative and administrative framework in place in India[12].

Changing discriminatory attitudes and practices against women which have been for so long deeply engrained, cannot be effected overnight, especially taking into consideration India's large size and complexity. For this region, a North-East Expert Committee has been recently constituted by the National Commission of Women, and it will focus on the problems of women and suggest strategies for their elimination. Violence against women does not only have a physical impact, but also has an impact on their ability to enjoy the full range of rights, including social, economic and political and the rights of women to enjoy the full range of rights is indivisible[13].

Rights are rarely self-evident, and usually stand in need of justification, and the justification seldom terminates in another assertion of right. And because the satisfaction of a right typically imposes costs on others, we need a mechanism for assigning responsibility for bearing those costs. Moreover, coercive intervention in any form is exceptional[14]. Women's rights in the context of drug and alcohol abuse may be viewed as rights accepted by all people consistently with acceptance of any of the main conceptions of political and economic justice in the world. It would be paternalistic to limit liberty on the grounds that those whole liberty is limited (women) would be better off as a result of the interference, and it would be unjustified, either because the subjects are capable of making choices for themselves or because the intervenor judges "better off" standards, the subjects have no reason to accept. The wide spread use of violence (drug/alcohol) against women in the home and community underlines the urgent need for steps to be taken to end this violence throughout society; and policies framed should be more than just rhetoric - they should firmly address ongoing problems of non-implementation, and or discriminatory implementation of safeguards and impunity for perpetrators of violence against women.

Strategies to Reduce Alcohol and Drug Related Violence Against Women

Women must first realize that the abuser wears many faces. Obvious forms of physical violence, like hitting or rough handling or using physical gestures of threatening a woman is just one power play men resort to. But the subtler forms of abuse need also to be addressed. Being frightened or isolated in your relationship, made to feel confused about your choices, disrespected, belittled, made to live in guilt, or have your confidence destroyed, being screamed at in front of friends and family, all or any one of these, if constantly at play in your relationship, are going to leave deep-emotional gashes. Does your partner, bend you out of shape to please him, 'allowing you' or 'disallowing' you to make free choices. No women should have to shape herself into a doormat to be walked over and crushed, to make reproductive choices against her will to have babies repeatedly or constant abortions or not be allowed to have a child. No woman should be forced to live in fear or ways not of her liking.

Recognizing that it is difficult for anybody most especially chronic alcoholics and drug users to give up alcohol/ drugs altogether, it would be beneficial to invest resources in the philosophy and practice of 'Harm Reduction'. This aims to decrease the adverse health, social and economic consequences of drug use without necessarily diminishing drug consumption.'(Wodak Saunders). This approach has gained increasing support over the last decade, while more conventional approaches have increasingly appeared ineffective, expensive and counter-productive. Examples of harm reduction include needle exchange to control the spread of HIV among injecting drug users (and consequently their partners as well), nicotine patches of tobacco users, and attempts to reduce physical injuries associated with alcohol intoxification by making environments in which people drink less dangerous. The Expert Committee of the World Health Organization commented, "In the harm minimisation approach, attention is directed to the careful scrutiny of all prevention and treatment strategies in terms of their intended and unintended effects on levels of drug-related harm"[15].

Although harm reduction is often misrepresented as a recent development in the alcohol and drug field, it has a long history. In ancient China, authorities attempted unsuccessfully to limit alcohol consumption as a means of preventing inebriated citizens falling into wintry canals freezing to death. Although it was not possible to eliminate public intoxication, the simple installation of barriers around canals was found to effectively prevent such deaths. Compulsory safety belt legislation was introduced in the 1860's in a number of countries when authorities became alarmed at the increasing numbers of alcohol-related road crash deaths. The action of the Nishabandhis and Meira Paibis although praiseworthy, has not been successful in curbing the use of alcohol and drugs and in preventing violence against women in Manipur. Harm Reduction also involves a substantial emphasis on human rights and a close partnership between law enforcement and health.

Reduction of drug-related harm (alcohol is included in this generic term) is a more logical target of state, national and international drug policy. Decreasing drug consumption is but one possible means of achieving this end. A contemporary division of harm reduction is supply reduction, demand reduction and harm reduction. Harm reduction implies the acceptance of incremental improvements, which are the best that particular individuals in particular circumstances can manage at particular times. A fundamental but poorly understood component of drug dependence is cycles of remission followed by relapse[16].

The most important strategy to reduce/eliminate alcohol and drug related violence against women, is to empower women. In the first instance, it means that every woman should be able to enjoy both self-esteem and self-respect, and mechanisms such as workshops to build up self-esteem/respect through the proper use of interpersonal skills, learning through the experiential method etc. need to be put in place. Economic independence is intimately linked with self-respect/esteem and measures to achieve this status need to be initiated especially for rural/illiterate women through non-formal education and vocational training, which is market-oriented. It needs to be reinforced that as women are in general excellent managers of money, a woman's personal income should be spent at her own discretion, and not arbitrarily taken away by the male head of the family. A proper understanding of women's rights and awareness, about the mechanisms to achieve redress, has to be put in place. Networking and communication between women's groups is a must, as also increasing men's involvement and responsibility towards women's well being. Research in the field of Gender and Masculinity is just an essential and a fresh orientation moving from violence against women to supportive practices. With gender-based violence on the increase, the search for solutions has gained momentum. There is a shift today in looking at men as a part of the solution, rather than only as perpetrators of violence. This necessitates the forging of meaningful partnerships between women and men. To enable concerted action against gender-based violence and discrimination, there is a need to focus on and learn more about masculinities and its various constructs[17]. The cycle of gender-based violence that was learned and passed down through each generation within the existing patriarchal system can be broken. Women's right to health in general, requires critical evaluation to ensure that women not only live longer, but are also in a position to protect themselves better, through their living years.

Because adolescence is a period of enormous and often stressful transition in a child's life in terms of physical and psychological development, counseling services must be provided to them, and it is through this medium that both adolescent girls and boys can be made aware of the necessity of doing away with gender-based violence especially if adolescent boys accept in practice, the equality of girls, concerted action can create a society that is gender equal and gender just, beneficial to women and men alike.

References

1. Action for Girls - Feb.2003-No.10 - Newsletter on NGO Working Group on Girls, New York.
2. Manipur is a high-prevalence State.
3. Manipur AIDS Control Society.
4. North East Publication 2001, Shillong.
5. *Outlook* - Anniversary Issue, August 2003.
6. UN AIDS - HIV/AIDS in India, 2000-2001

7. Rapid Situation Assessment of Drug Use in Imphal (1999-2000) - Kripa Society, Imphal.
8. Drug Addiction in North East India - Salam Irene (paper, 1996).
9. Intervention for Drug Users - Salam Irene (paper, 2000).
10. Women, Children, Increasingly Fall Victim to HIV/AIDS - Julie Subha, Imphal Free Press, March 22nd 2003.
11. Amnesty International India - The Impact of Violence Against Women, May 2001.
12. Ibid.
13. Ibid.
14. Human Rights as a Common Concern - *The American Political Science Review,* Menusha, June 2001 - Charles R. Beitz
15. Harm Reduction as an Approach to Treatment - Dr. Alex Wodak (paper, 2000)
16. Ibid.
17. From Violence to Supportive Practices - Chandini Joshi, UNIFEM, Delhi 2003.

6

'THE SEEN' AND 'THE UNSEEN'
Sociological Dimensions to Violence against Women in Manipur

—N. Vijaylakshmi Brara

INTRODUCTION

War, conflict and aggression have traditionally been associated with men. Many sociologists studying symbolism say that even the shape of the bullet, and its piercing the body has a lot of maleness about it. Rape and wife battering then form a miniscule part of such acculturated notions. Women in such paradigm then become receivers, sufferers and the most effected. When, consequently, the state becomes the aggressor it is the same women who are at the receiving end and the most aggrieved.

What we see in the rest of India is the organizations of women, which are raising their voices against the aggression of the first kind. And what we see in Manipur is the struggle of Manipuri women against the oppressive forces of the state as well as the non-state/private groups who shake the edifice of their society. They have been looking beyond individuals and they hold themselves responsible to maintain the order in their society. But they have not yet raised their heads to look whether this order of the society, which they feel responsible to uphold, is egalitarian, non-paternalist and non-exploitative *vis-à-vis* their own standing.

The General Scenario

The Visible Groups

In the present scenario we have strong women's front in every community in Manipur. Among the Meitei community (the valley based) it is the Meira-Paibies, the Naga Women's Union among the Nagas, the Kuki Women's Association, Lamkang Women's Union, Moyon Women's Union, Chothe Women's Union, Tangkhul Shanao Long etc. among the various other hill tribes. In short we have organized women's force in each tribe and community.

The 'Meira Paibis' are the torch-bearing women. They hold Mashaals (torch) and roam in the locality to keep a watch on drunkenness and drug-abuse. They are also protectors of the people against the repressive acts of the armed forces. They make a human wall in cases where innocent local youths are forcibly being taken away by the armed forces in the name of containing insurgents. They are the only ones who dare to warn and scold the people in under-ground movement for their excesses. Everybody is cautious of them. They dare to get lathi charged, to sit for hunger strikes and even go to jail for a right cause.

So are the women's groups in the hills. The Naga Mother's Association (NMA) and the Kuki Women's Association (KWA) and other women's groups of the various other tribes are the guardians of their respective tribes. They played a pivotal role during Naga-Kuki clashes, where barbarism of the worst kind got unleashed in its naked proportions in the name of ethnic cleansing. Even infants were beheaded. It was at that moment that NMA and KWA went hand in hand long stretches in the hills (sometimes walking 3-4 days continuously) to meet their respective under-ground outfits to tell them to stop killing each other.

The major activities of these women's groups in the hills include going from village to village preaching about peace and harmony, conducting fasting programmes to end the ethnic clashes, condemning, protesting and demanding compensation and judicial enquiry into killing of innocent villagers by the security forces. At the same time like the Meira-Paibies, they stand against the drug abuse, prostitution, alcoholism, gambling and the vices affecting their society.

Manipuri women's groups are the watch-dogs of their society. They are the mothers. Like any other mother they can go to any extent to safeguard the lives and interests of their children and their society. Nowhere else, will one find such vast network of organizations of women. Their handling of the most difficult situations in most non-violent ways is remarkable. They are a treasure in themselves. Their organizational skills and their non-violent means even in the face of barbaric violence can be a wonderful learning and sharing experience within the South Asian region.

Women in Manipur are very visible. Besides these socio-political groupings mentioned above, we are also very proud of exclusive women's market called the 'Ima Keithel'. The women here are mostly vegetable vendors and cloth merchants who mostly sell their own produce. No man is allowed to establish his shop here. These market vendors also have a very strong organization. The police are afraid to hassle them. Long time ago, when I was in Delhi, I saw a play about how the Ima-Keithel women successfully protested against their area being converted into a multi-storey building. Presently, the agitation is revived and one can again see them in strength sitting in dharna outside their sheds. If one goes through the history of Manipur it was the Ima-Keithel, which was the launching pad of the two-epoch making Nupi Lals (women's fights). It was here where they organized and pursued their movements and fought against the colonial forces. It is not only an economic base of the Imaș, but also their political base.

Formal Political Arena-trying to be Visible

The women's associations are very strong and powerful bodies. But one also notices that empowerment of women, however, is miserably inadequate considering the tremendous works done by them. The representation of women in Panchayat, Zilla Parishad etc. has not cut much ice as the women representations cannot come out of the corrupt political culture, thus diminishing their effectiveness in these institutions. There is a lone woman MLA in the entire 60-member legislative assembly. In reverse to that we have very impressive representation of women in the lower rung of our democratic institutions. In fact, we often cross the 33% reservations granted to the women, where some women are able to get elected from non-reserved seats. But, it has not changed the scenario. They are struggling to acquire their legitimate power from the patriarchal state machinery and even within the family.

During my long work with the women panchayat members I was often reminded of the film 'The God Mother', in which actress Shabana Azmi rises from a submissive wife to a powerful politician. She rises in her position through various rigors of 'dirty politics' and in the process she herself becomes a power hungry, corrupt and sadistic person. But what happens in the end? She saves the life of a woman whom her own son wants to forcefully marry even paying with her own life. She went through a process whereby she did what most of the male politicians at her genre did and then finally emerged as a woman with her own mind. OK, so what, after all its only a film. So let's go to the real world.

Atombi Devi (name changed) is an upa-gram pradhan. Her husband is a drunkard. He really troubles her. But in his presence she has to say that he fully supports her. Her son was killed by the security forces few years back. Yet, inspite of such hardships, she is vigorously working for the development of the area. Shanti (name changed) is a gram pradhan. Her husband always takes over from her even in her official meetings. His interference is such a nuisance for the villagers that it may hamper her future electoral prospects. Yet she lets him to take the lead. She has no choice. There is another woman gram pradhan by the name Laila (name changed) who was also a member of the local Meira Paibi group. But her pradhanship, which was seen as her entry into official politics was completely denounced by her husband and sons. They even threatened to leave the house if she contested another election. Recently, I invited one-gram pradhan of a panchayat in Assam for a meeting in Delhi. She hesitated and told me that she should take permission from her husband and also her son for going to Delhi! Talk about devolution of power!

The husbands are often seen trying to influence their wife members. I have been noticing this especially when I am in conversation with the women pradhans. Both the women pradhans and I have learnt to simply nod our heads (we dare not ignore their opinions) and carry on with our discussions. In the other parts of India, a term has been coined for them—Pradhanpati (Pradhan's husband). These unofficial pradhans are much more powerful than the official pradhans themselves. In one of the meetings hosted by Najma Heptullah in honour of women panchayat leaders across the country, many of them voiced unanimously "we can do better if we are not restricted by our male colleagues, male members of the family and bureaucracy."

The women members whom I have been interacting in the field are socially very active. The reservation of the offices of the pradhan and up-pradhan for women has ensured their participation in the affairs of the village. In their official capacity they are effective. Some people in a village told us that women are considered more sincere, less corrupt and less quarrelsome than the male members. The fact that some of them initially are part of the Meira-Paibi movement that gives their curriculum-vitae a facelift. But we should not forget that they are also 'soft targets'. They are marginalized in all spheres of life specially in education and an overwhelming Chatnabis (societal rules) hovering around her telling her that no matter what, her husband and her household come first. Bureaucrats do not take them seriously and the MLAs have a 'Karino Ibemaa' (what is the matter, dear girl) attitude with lighthearted mannerism. In the backdrop of all so strong Meira-Paibies movements one also cannot help overhearing remarks like, "What can a woman do?" or "A woman should look after her children and home rather than running here and there". If asked to comment on the woman zilla adhayaksha, a smirk comes on people's faces that evade by saying that a "Boss is a Boss". Then there are actually those people who claim that a male adhayaksha is an obvious choice for the people. If reservation has to be given then two posts of adhayaksha should be created - one male and another female! Isn't our Prime Minister mooting this idea too? He mentioned in his Independence Day speech that the reservation bill in the parliament will get an easy acceptance if there is a provision of dual membership- one male and another female!

Now, let us also try to reach the higher power block - the legislature. We have numerous examples of women MLAs/ MPs. Some are prominent and some are not so prominent as in other parts of the country. Here we have to realize that most of these are the women who, because of their family backgrounds, did not have to struggle their ways into the political arena. Therefore, they are neither marginalized nor taken lightly because of their 'connections'. But they still work under the paradigms set by the male patriarchs. In fact, Indira Gandhi felt proud when on one occasion she was declared the only 'man' in the Parliament. She even criticized the airhostesses saying that they are not 'attractive'. Most of the women politicians are conscious of not upsetting the traditional role model of women. In other words, not only our women who have barely managed to reach the lower rungs of the governance but also the top women politicians of our country have to work under the Chatnabis (social rules) of their respective patriarchies.

Coming back to the Meira paibis, most of these women are naive and innocent. They work on their instincts. So, whoever can trigger their motherly emotions can get them on their side. This kind of instinctive reaction comes in the way of their role as watchdogs. That is the reason why, inspite of such a strong body, we do not have any leaders among them - leaders of reckoning, not only of the Meira Paibis but also a leader of the whole society.

Of Women should not be presumed as for women:

Another problem with these groups as I perceive is that these women are reluctant to rock the social norms of the society. They do not address it. Neither do they have any policy nor any ideology towards domestic violence, polygamous liaisons and other male generated violence, which are prevalent in our societies. Neither do they address to the women's issues in general. They are the organizations only of women but not necessarily for women.

A vacuum in this area was felt very strongly, especially, when I heard the story of Nisha Sharma, a young woman from Noida, Delhi, who handed over her would-have-been husband to the police. I started wondering. Are we in Manipur different? Perhaps yes, but only a bit. We do not demand dowry openly. We do not beat the bride's father. But don't we taunt and humiliate the new bride if she has not brought what we expected? To further my argument let me cite some incidents that I came across during my fieldwork. I will cite two/three recent incidents to clarify my point. One woman fully established in her profession married a man in the age, which we generally call "late marriage". After a long gap she conceived but had a daughter. The boy's mother convinced him to get married again to have a son! The wife considering her status felt extremely humiliated. She went to the local Meira-paibis to complain. But this is how they reacted, "A man can marry four-five times, so what if he is marrying another one." After sometime, the second wife, half his age, also delivered a baby girl. But that's another story. The second incident also relates to the polygamous liaison, but in this case nobody including the wife was objecting to the second marriage. The Meira-paibis were instead impressing upon the husband to give some property to the first wife. The husband getting another wife was not even considered worth discussing. It is high time the Meira Paibis have a serious look into this continuing social practice. We have been witnessing of late the domestic conflicts because of polygamy. Only a few days back there was this report of the wife having four children pouring kerosene over her self and trying to immolate herself devastated over her husband's eloping with another woman.

There was yet another incident, which is related to a dictum passed by an under-ground outfit directing Manipuri women to wear only their traditional dress. One girl not taking it seriously went about in a salwar-kameez. Some men very rudely remarked her in the public. The local Meira-paibis reacted to it by scolding the girl as to why she simply could not obey and wear the traditional dress.

It seems here that the Meira-paibis' predominant role in our society is to see that peace and social order is maintained. They are yet to adopt the role of challenging the social customs which are loaded with gender biases and fight for an egalitarian social set-up. The Chatnabis or the social norms are upheld even when they are not women-friendly. Any anormative behavior that goes against the social customs is discouraged and denounced. The traditions and the customs are not challenged and, according to them, not meant to be challenged.

In the socio-political sphere we have the "Meira-Paibis": in the economic sphere we have the Ima-Keithel. If we look at these two public spheres, which generally the social scientists have tended to do, then one gets a picture that the status of Manipuri women is indeed very high because of their high visibility in the public sphere. But are these the only indices through which one can and should analyze the status? Is visibility in public sphere the only criteria?

What about the Domestic Sphere?

What about the social norms as mentioned earlier? True, we do not have female infanticides, dowry deaths, rape and molestation. (But wait! haven't we started witnessing the last two, of late?). Our Niyams are very subtly laid, brushed under the carpet, wrapped with 'ceremonialities', therefore, difficult to pinpoint and therefore difficult to denounce.

The Subtle Norms : The Unseen

Women, who is married through proper rituals and has a first born son can only lead the ritual procession of marriage or of the 6th day celebration of the birth of the child or on any other auspicious occasion. It is considered inauspicious if a woman who had married through elopement and does not have an issue or has only a girl child, to hold the gifts of any ritual occasion.

When a girl is born, it is not as catastrophic as probably in the Hindi belt, yet, it brings sympathy from the people, when invariably everybody would say, 'doesn't matter, try for a boy next time'. The pundit in the Swasthipujah ceremony of the girl child holds a ceremony of propitiating the god to "gift" a son next time.

Behavior patterns of the girl child and the boy child are also very clearly defined. A girl child is supposed to be obedient, soft spoken and play quietly. A loud behavior, shouting and jumping is remarked as 'nang nupa raa"? (Are you a boy?). I remember an incident where a small girl wanting to fly a kite was carrying one in her hand. Around 2-3 people whom she met on the way asked her, "Nupi na telanga paibra" (does a girl fly kite?). Needless to say she reached home depressed and confused. The societal behaviour pattern had already condemned her to her expected role. It is here that the oppression starts. Similarly to a boy who is coy and shy, people say he should have been a girl. Contrary to the aggressive image in public in the form of Meira-paibis, submissiveness in the domestic sphere is approved, accepted and desired by the society and even in the face of an aggressive and violent male.

The Meitei marriage ceremony is the embodiment of subjugation of woman by her husband. The term for husband is mapuroiba, which means the master. During the marriage ceremony the bride has to go around the bridegroom and shower flowers on him after each round. Although, the boy's family and the girl's family do not stand in a rigid hierarchy as seen in the mainland, there are certain ritual roles which connote a certain superior status to the boy's family. The newly wed girl is expected to involve herself in domestic chores the moment she enters the groom's house and when all the guests leave. The very next day she is expected to get up before sunrise and take the reigns of household work. When she delivers a child, it is the mother and other women of her natal home who will be responsible for post natal and child-care. That includes washing all the soiled clothes and cooking the food separately for her, since she as well as her child is under birth pollution for the period of 12 days. Till that time the boy's family will not touch the girl or the child while it is considered all right for the girl's side to contract defilement.

The ritual position of the women in the social gatherings as well as at home is the left side, while the right side is reserved for the men. Social anthropologists would be familiar with the concepts of left and right as propounded by Mary Douglas in her book "Purity and Danger." Left is associated with impurity, defilement, death and women, while purity, auspiciousness, life and men symbolize right. The seating arrangement in the famous Lai Haraoba ceremony (pleasing the deity) or any other public function is based on the similar principle. In the bedroom, the husband sleeps on the right side of the bed. The daughters' room is in the left side of the traditional Meitei household structure. The dead body, which brings defilement, is taken out from the left side of the house.

The role of younger women within the family structure is seen exclusively in the realm of Leishabi (unmarried, marriageable daughter) and Mou (the daughter-in-law). Therefore, if you are neither, people cannot define your position in the society. Women, who decide not to marry and cross the 'age', cannot be defined in any terminological category. In any ritual occasion, the functions and duties are specified for the Leishabies and the mous. The women, who are beyond marriageable age and yet not married, do not know their exact position in the whole set-up. Interestingly, women belonging to such category are increasing in the Meitei social set-up. There are many women, who are professionals and very well established as doctors, journalists, lawyers etc and who are finding it difficult to adjust with the unchanging norms of their society. They say that a mou's role is too demanding. No matter what one is at the professional level, as an ideal mou, one has to get up at 4 a.m., sweep the floor, take a bath, pray, and then enter the kitchen to cook, then deliver a baby (preferably a son) within a year and uphold all the family rituals and gatherings in priority to one's job. It is this group of women who have now started struggling with patriarchal notions and demanding in their own way for an egalitarian society. I have often seen them either organizing or attending seminars related to topics such as 'Women and AIDS', 'Harassment at work place', 'Women and health' etc. In other words they seem to have started to take up the mantle of bringing forth women's issues in the forefront in the Meitei society.

One may question at this point, as to how a society that on the whole encourages economic independence with exclusive 'Ima Keithel', can build such an attitude towards professional working women. Let me try to dwell on this problem. The concept of economic independence is there in terms of Ima Keithel as long as the younger Mous (daughters-in-law) are there to look after the household chores. It is the elder women who generally used to run such Keithel. A generational continuity used to be maintained to keep a balance between the domesticity and the Keithel. Therefore, the social and domestic order was not disturbed. But now, when the women (who are generally young) have professional jobs, the house routine and the established division of labour are disturbed giving rise to turmoil in the domestic fronts. To avoid such tensions and seeing the experiences of their friends many are now refraining from marrying. It is not that women are not encouraged to work in offices, but we will find very few of them occupying the higher responsible posts. They are mostly in the lower ranks, where there is not much demand from their job. So that they can also look after the household, which is after 'their entire job'.The division of labour is very clearly classified and is very rigid. I remember an incident, where in a kitchen of one household I jokingly asked an unmarried man to cook some dish, immediately his sister came running and said, " why should he cook, has his sister died?"

Polygamy and wife beating, which are closely related, surprisingly increased over a period of time. So have the incidences of rape. Rape, which was unheard of a few years ago, has started showing its ugly heads. Recently there was a case where the security guards of the High Court were caught red handed trying to rape two young girls in the High Court premises! They were nabbed. Thanks to the timely intervention by some news reporters. Men in Manipur attach prestige to the fact of their having more than one wife. Reasons can range from the first wife having no issue, having only daughters, started looking old, and he somehow likes the hair of the other girl. Nobody can challenge his position, not even in the court, since the second or third wives never actually get legally married. However, their children have the legitimate rights over his property. Since aggressive behaviour is expected from a male member, wife beating too is not condoned. It is often said that she must have provoked him to do so. A mere whimper of protest from the woman entails a threat of the husband getting a second wife. Now a days, we are hearing some sounds of protests from the women folk. Unfortunately, they are showing their displeasure by harming themselves. I have already cited an incident of a woman burning herself with kerosene. We do not have any state commission for women nor any redressal forum exclusively geared up to deal with such crises. A woman in such a situation is left alone. All the social norms are also against her. We do not have a 'seen' and visible purdah in our society but there is an all-pervasive 'unseen' purdah enveloping the whole ethos of the women's existence. It is indeed a frightening situation.

Hill Women - Tradition Bound

The main hurdle I feel among the hill tribes of Manipur in the empowerment in domestic as well as in political front is the customary laws. Here I want to share an incident, which happened in a remote village where I had gone to conduct a gender workshop. After listening to me for one hour one participant said, "But madam we are convinced of the fact that women are physically and mentally weak! There will not be any peace if the women are given equal status." They were apprehensive of empowering women in the local bodies saying that, "then who will look after the house? They will refuse to respect us." On my suggestion to start sharing the domestic chores with their wives, they had a fit of laughter.

In the hills, the drudgery of the work done by women is stark. There is 'iron bar' rigidity in the division of labour. The women bear on an average[6] children and with no health centers their health deteriorates with every delivery. They collect wood, cook food, weave clothes for the family, go to the fields and take care of the children. They work quietly and are invisible in any decision-making bodies.

According to Valley Rose, a Tangkhul woman leader and a journalist, "women were considered secondary citizens in the society. Head counts are made only on the male members. Women are not allowed to speak out for theirselves in front of the male folks (especially elders). Women are not allowed to represent in the grass root administration i.e. Village authority or Council. Male folk have the freedom to practise polygamy whereas women are charged and judged with adultery if she is found to be having extra-marital affairs with another man." According to Naga customary laws women do not have the right to inherit parents' properties. Divorce compounds the miseries. According to Dolly Kikon, a member of the Naga Peoples' Movement for Human Rights, the in-laws send women away from their marital homes on the death of their husbands if they have no children to 'look' after. A widow is denied of the right to get her deceased husband's pension funds. According to her, "some Naga men today vent out their frustration by telling women that no matter what educational qualification she possesses or even if she goes to the moon and comes back, she will end up washing her husband's undergarments and wash his posterior after he defecates." Even in the majority of the Kuki tribes if a woman does not have a son, inheritance by the wife and daughters is impossible. The widow has followed the commands of the male inheritor who then has the custody of the children as well as the property along with the pension of her husband. The Naga Women's Union as well as the Kuki women are fighting hard to amend their customary laws, since they feel them as effective tools to victimize the women without justification by the male patriarchs of their society.

There is a very interesting argument mooted in defense of the customs and traditions of our Manipuri society as a whole and that is we are far better off than our counterparts in the mainland India where women are not even allowed to be born and where female infanticide and bride burning are regular features. This attempt to shut us down with attempts to compare degrees of oppression entails further problems. The subtle codes in the garb of rigid social norms defying us to live our lives with dignity are more difficult to handle than the stark and bold discriminatory practices of the mainland Indians.

I have asserted time and again that the customs and the laws enforced by our forefathers are fantastic in helping to maintain the identity of our different ethnic groups but they need to change and amend along with the changing times. Women of repute of our respective tribes should be consulted with to make our customary laws more egalitarian and gender sensitive. The main area of focus should be polygamy, divorce and property rights, and the sphere where injustices against women are most pronounced. We have also to realize that nothing remains static, and if we do not change with times then our customs will be fossilized and washed out by relentless forces of change and along with it, its positive aspects. This will definitely not augur well for our unique heritage. We have to realize and accept that even the Constitution of India has had to be amended time and again.

The Inside and the Outside

If we look quite closely, we will realize that the Manipuri women simultaneously live in two different worlds - the inside and the outside. Their 'outside' image is that of a vigorous, organized force fighting for justice and the caretaker of the society. While in their inside world the traits such as submissiveness and subservience are the accepted behaviour. Inside their homes their male relations, specially the husbands become their caretakers. There are cases where a woman who is thrashing a drunkard on the road and is applauded for the act accepts beating by her drunkard husband at home. And if she protests then there will be no accolades at home or by the society around her. The social scientists while studying this society have mostly concentrated on the outside world whereas the inside world has been left ignored. This has led to the belief that the status of Manipuri women is high.

While saying this, I would not also deny that there are indeed certain progressive elements in this society. The women are given space to earn their living. They have full ownership on their dowry, which is returned after the divorce, if a woman is widowed or divorced among the Meities. She is given a landed property by her natal home. In other words, she never breaks her tie with her parents' home. She remains their Ningol (daughter). Probably our hill sisters have to struggle much more in terms of inheritance. Incidents such as sati, dowry-deaths and female infanticide are absent in this society.

Some reflections

We, in the Northeast have been witnessing the longest struggle against the repression by state agencies. We have been too engrossed with the atrocities committed on us by the security forces. The women in trying to save the lives of their children and their men folk have not yet been able to focus their attention to the crude as well as the subtle violence meted out to them even though they are the worst victims in such a situation. They are sexually targeted both by the state and the underground outfits. They have been victims of mental, physical and sexual violences. It has been estimated that three to four out of ten rape cases go unreported. An incident where the woman was raped by a security personnel right in front of his 8 years old handicapped son is still fresh in our minds. The infamous Oinam (name of a Poumei village) incident where the pregnant woman was compelled to deliver in the fields has become part of our nightmare. Imagine the extent of mental torture these women undergo when their sons are simply picked up and disappear. In our list of priorities, probably peace comes first and the egalitarian concepts, encompassing dignity and respect will probably come much later. I have yet to come across a pressure group fighting for the dignity of the women in such situations. It is unfortunate but true that the issues of rape/ molestation are obscured, sidelined and marginalized for the "greater" cause of nationhood and self-determination. Our women had, therefore, no time to concentrate on their own plight. They have been always ready and organized to follow the commands of their male leaders. The women themselves have never looked at themselves and their inside worlds.

Hence, if one is looking for overt, blatant, crude form of sexual discrimination and threat to existence of women, we shall not find it in this society. But, does that mean that the discrimination is not there? Are we allowed to live a life of dignity with no imposition of inferior status? No, the discrimination is there, but in a subtle form, which does not make it less serious. No body stops us but we feel bound by our Chatnabis, the rigid social norms, the customary laws and traditions. The warning word in Meitei is touhoide (not supposed to be done) and we cannot question it. Many of us have experienced this when we have dared to say or do something different. In fact, this makes the task of a researcher as well as of a social activist very difficult. Since, one is setting out to research something, which is apparently not there. An activist is seeing it happening but cannot pinpoint at the issue. One has to, therefore, look inside, into the homes, the gestures, the unsaid codes, the meaning of various phrases, the decision-making in the family, the prescriptions on dress codes and behavior etc, to understand this kind of discrimination and oppression.

The Basic Approach

Mere socio-political level is, therefore, not enough to understand the level of status of women in this society. The notion of patriarchy has to be understood first not as system but as a concept, as a dominant idea, as a hagemonizing principle in any society. Patriarchy, when seen as a concept pervades the whole ethos of the society. The whole society emanates a common idea that man is superior. It may be in a direct, crude form or in an indirect and subtle form. And I have yet to come across a society where this ethos is completely absent. The status of women is, therefore, never very high. To understand this, one has to observe the rites of passage, the man-woman relationship, the commonly used proverbs, the division of labour, the role expectations, the rituals, the forms of addresses, the behaviour pattern, and other such miniscule concepts. The variables have to be different from when we study, for example, the class struggle, the caste system or the relevance of various 'ism', where the study of socio-political and economic aspects gives a somewhat holistic understanding.

My belief is that, as long as Patriarchy remains an all-pervading concept in a given social system, be it partilineal, matrilineal, patri-local or matrilocal, 'modern' or 'traditional', women's status will remain more or less the same in all these societies although the variables leading to their status may differ. In the conflict situation such as in Manipur, war, aggression, violence and revivalism of traditional value system go hand in hand and further reinforce the notions of patriarchy.

The Conflict Situation

The trend is emerging in Manipur, where we see that the educated women have started questioning the existing norms. But given in any war situation, the agenda of looking for insides of any society does not become part of the agenda of the leaders from either side. In a conflict situation, when one is espousing and dying for the cause of 'freeing' the 'motherland', gender sensitivity becomes a neglected arena even a selfish and distracting thought and consequently the issue gets further marginalized. We, I think, have to come out of this war situation first to be able to concentrate, to understand how oppressive and gender insensitive our inside dwellings are.

Right now we are struggling with the questions of 'identity', 'nationalism', 'sub-nationalism' and 'self-determination'. Violence against women, especially domestic violence is not the prime agènda. It is still seen as a private affair of an individual and of the household. Therefore, we have not been able to have a social platform for it. In other words, it has to come from 'inside' to the 'outside', from personal to public and from the 'unseen' to the 'seen'.

References

Brara. N.Vijaylakshmi. 1998, Politics, Society and Cosmology in India's North East, OUP, Delhi,

Douglas, Mary.1985, Purity and Danger, Ark Paperbacks, Boston.

Fernandes, Walter et.el.2002. Changing women's status in India: Focus on the Northeast, Northeast Social Research Centre, Guwahati.

Hodson, T.C. 1989.The Meitheis, Low Price Publications, Delhi.

Kikon, Dolly. (Un-published paper) Political Mobilization of Women in Nagaland: A Sociological Background.

Leslie, Julia.I, 1989. The Perfect Wife, OUP.

Parret, Saroj Nalini, 1980 The Religion of Manipur, Firma Klm Private Limited, Calcutta.

Raisunriang, 1998. 4th issue Naga Women's Union, Manipur.

Sircar, Manjusri Chaki.1984, Feminism in a Traditional Society, Shakti Books, Gaziabad, U.P.

7

Violence against Women in Tripura

—Minakshi Sen Bandyopadhyay

INTRODUCTION

Violence against women is a global phenomenon and it is rising in India. It is reported that "Crime against women are on the rise, along with crime in general". Tripura is not an exception. Available data show that reported crimes against women are at a rise in Tripura (Table 7.1).

The rise of crime against women generally in India " is due to at least in part to what is now described as the criminalisation of politics". Among the criminal groups thus involved are the urban mafias, the rural senas, those behind smuggling liquor, drugs and protection rackets and so on. The brunt of the resulting violence is born by the marginalized section of the society viz. women in particular. But in Tripura all those factors mentioned above which resulted in the rise of violence against women are not present. Some factors are common, but some major factors mentioned above are totally absent. Yet, reported crimes against women are on the rise in Tripura.

As per data recorded by NCRB (National Crime Board Bureau), 1995-1997, the crime rate in general is low in

Tripura compared to other states of India. But peculiarly enough crime rates against women are quite high in Tripura. In the light of those recorded data of NCRB and data recorded by Tripura Police before and after 1997 up to 2002 and the cases registered in TCW (Tripura Commission for Women), a very active statuary body engaging in the work for protection and empowerment of women in the state, author is trying to present the actual position of crime against women in Tripura (Tables 7.1 to 7.3).

Table 7.1

STATES AND UNION TERRITORIES IN ASCENDING ORDER OF TOTAL CRIME RATE

(per million persons)

Low		Upper-Middle	
1. Lakshadweep	571.96	17. Arunachal Pradesh	1885.22
2. Punjab	600.68	18. Himachal Pradesh	1888.12
3. West Bengal	895.49	19. Maharashtra	2137.12
4. Meghalaya	916.52	20. Tamil Nadu	2224.07
5. Nagaland	941.76	21. Daman & Deiu	2354.65
6. Uttar Pradesh	1077.85	22. Karnataka	2356.42
7. Tripura	1129.63	23. Goa	2444.30
8. Bihar	1216.86	24. Dadra & Nagar Haveli	2499.04
Lower-Middle		**High**	
9. Andaman & Nicobar	1285.93	25. Gujarat	2635.19
10. Manipur	1301.52	26. Pondicherry	2646.55
11. Jammu & Kashmir	1402.22	27. Madhya Pradesh	2683.35
12. Sikkim	1425.95	28. Chandigarh	2734.43
13. Assam	1463.32	29. Mizoram	2769.75
14. Orissa	1470.25	30. Kerala	2850.08
15. Andhra Pradesh	1484.82	31. Rajasthan	3168.49
16. Haryana	1787.25	32. Delhi	4863.29

Table 7.2
STATES AND UNION TERRITORIES IN ASCENDING ORDER OF TOTAL CRIME RATE AGAINST WOMEN

(per million persons)

Low		Upper -Middle	
1. Lakshadweep	0.00	17. Chandigarh	92.15
2. Daman & Deiu	7.48	18. Kerala	95.76
3. Nagaland	25.26	19. Tripura	99.11
4. Meghalaya	29.88	20. Jammu & Kashmir	101.01
5. Pondicherry	31.83	21. Orissa	110.35
6. Punjab	35.81	22. Dadra & Nagar Haveli	111.02
7. Bihar	39.98	23. Sikkim	114.60
8. Manipur	44.59	24. Assam	118.78
Lower -Middle		**High**	
9. Goa	50.54	25. Haryana	119.41
10. Tamil Nadu	72.03	26. Andhra Pradesh	121.97
11. Karnataka	74.51	27. Mizoram	127.89
12. Andaman & Nicobar	75.18	28. Himachal Pradesh	139.42
13. Uttar Pradesh	77.40	29. Maharashtra	173.81
14. West Bengal	86.77	30. Delhi	197.14
15. Gujarat	89.27	31. Madhya Pradesh	206.97
16. Arunachal Pradesh	91.78	32. Rajasthan	208.16

The above tables directly quoted form the paper written by Chandan Mukherjee, P. Rastogi and N. Krishnajee (*Economic and Political Weekly*, Oct. 27th, 2001), indicate the position of Tripura in respect of total crime scenario in the Indian states and the position of Tripura in respect of crime against women. As per their analysis, Delhi, Kerala, Mizoram and Pondicherry are in the high crime category. The other in this group includes Rajasthan, M.P., Gujarat and U.P., Chandigarh. And the 'low' crime category states include Tripura, Punjab, West Bengal, U.P., Nagaland, Meghalaya and Bihar. While in case of Tripura, it is obvious that general

Table 7.3

DISTRIBUTION OF STATES/UTs BY LEVEL OF TOTAL CRIME RATE AND CRIME RATE AGAINST WOMEN

Total Crime Rate		Crime	Rate	Against Women
	Low	Lower-Middle	Upper-Middle	High
	Lakshadweep Punjab Meghalaya Nagaland Bihar	West Bengal Uttar Pradesh	Tripura	
Lower Middle	Manipur	Andaman & Nicobar	Jammu and Kashmir Sikkim Assam Orissa	Andhra Pradesh Haryana
Upper-Middle	Daman & Deiu	Arunachal -Pradesh Tamil Nadu Karnataka Goa	Dadra & Nagar Haveli	Himachal Pradesh Maharashtra
High	Pondichery	Gujarat	Chandigarh Kerala	Madhya Pradesh Mizoram Rajasthan Delhi

crime rate (excluding extremist violence) is very low but in case of Bihar and U.P., the crime rate appears to be too low to be credible. On the other hand, the authors observed that crime against women (as per NCRB data) is very high in Delhi, M.P., Rajasthan, Himachal Pradesh, Haryana, A.P., Mizoram, Maharashtra etc. It is notable that all those states, which are big, are especially prone to crime against women.

But there is a common conception that CAW (Crime against women) is directly associated with overall crime. And it is true that there seems to be a correspondence between them. But, Tripura, M.P. and Haryana are exception. In A.P. and Haryana, the crime rate is categorized in lower middle group. In Tripura, crime rate is low. But all the three states are notably exception of the common inference that CAW is associated with overall crime rate.

On the other hand, exceptions are Daman, Diu, Pondicherry and Gujarat. On available date collected form Tripura Police (CID) and from the data of registered cases in TCW, I will try to say something about my understanding on high CAW in Tripura in the background of low overall crime rate.

Data Collected from Tripura Police

Table 7.4

DETAILS OF CASES ON DOMESTIC/EXTREMIST VIOLENCE AND RAPE CASE REGISTERED IN WEST DIST. DURING THE PERIOD FROM 1994 TO 30.04.2003

	NO. OF CASES REGISTERED		DIFFERENT P.S.
YEAR	DOMESTIC VIOLENCE	RAPE	EXTREMIST VIOLENCE UPON WOMEN
1994	19	26	2
1995	34	33	N/A
1996	42	23	N/A
1997	30	23	3
1998	19	17	1
1999	23	17	1
2000	40	27	3
2001	80	25	2
2002	76	44	3
2003 upto 30.04.03	34	10	2

Table 7.5

DETAILS OF CASES ON DOMESTIC /EXTREMIST VIOLENCE AND RAPE CASE REGISTERED IN SOUTH DIST. DURING THE PERIOD FROM 1994 TO 30.04.03.

No. of	Cases Regd	In	DIFFERENT P.S.
YEAR	DOMESTIC VIOLENCE	RAPE	EXTREMIST VIOLENCE UPON WOMEN
1994	12	16	1
1995	23	25	N/A
1996	27	30	N/A
1997	32	32	N/A
1998	40	22	N/A
1999	53	28	N/A
2000	43	36	N/A
2001	62	29	1
2002	91	30	2
2003 upto 30.04.03	14	06	N/A

Table 7.6

DETAILS OF CASES ON DOMESTIC /EXTREMIST VIOLENCE AND RAPE CASE REGISTERED IN NORTH DIST. DURING THE PERIOD FROM 1994 TO 30.04.03.

NO. OF YEAR	CASES REGD DOMESTIC VIOLENCE	IN RAPE	DIFFERENT P.S. EXTREMIST VIOLENCE UPON WOMEN
1994	09	19	4
1995	11	24	2
1996	7	22	4
1997	10	26	2
1998	12	10	3
1999	08	22	6
2000	10	17	1
2001	09	28	1
2002	06	33	N/A
2003 upto 30.04.03	01	08	1

Table 7.7

CASES PEGISTERED IN TRIPURA COMMISSION FOR WOMEN IN 2002-03

DIST.	Total complaints	Bride Killing	Bigamy	Extra Marital Relation	Other domestic violence	Rape	Others	Send to police for proper action	Send to court for proper action	Summon in commission court for Counseling and Mitigation
WEST	466	22	41	12	299	20	60	106	13	338
NORTH	38	2	3	4	19	2	7	15	N/A	14
SOUTH	74	4	2	5	44	7	10	36	N/A	29
DHALAI	18	1	3	4	8	1	1	11	N/A	6
TOTAL	596	29	49	25	370	30	84	168	13	387

Table 7.8

CASES REGISTERED IN TRIPURA COMMISSION FOR WOMEN IN 2002

DIST.	Total complaints	Bride Killing	Bigamy	Extra Marital Relation	Other domestic violence	Rape	Others	Send to police for proper action	Send to court for proper action	Summon in commission for Counseling and Mitigation
WEST	519	27	44	18	319	19	92	97	11	400
NORTH	39	1	3	3	21	2	9	16	N/A	14
SOUTH	78	3	4	6	48	6	11	29	N/A	40
DHALAI	21	1	N/A	2	13	1	1	9	N/A	11
TOTAL	657	32	51	29	401	28	113	151	11	465

Table 7.9

CASES REGESTERED IN TRIPURA COMMISSION FOR WOMEN IN 2001

DIST.	Total complaints	Bride Killing	Bigamy	Extra Marital Relation	Other domestic violence	Rape	Others	Send to police for proper action	Send to court for proper action	Summon in commission for Counseling and Mitigation
WEST	389	23	9	7	309	8	33	90	12	281
NORTH	44	2	9	4	31	1	6	22	N/A	9
SOUTH	92	5	8	8	55	3	13	52	N/A	28
DHALAI	20	1	2	6	10	1	N/A	10	2	5
TOTAL	545	31	20	25	405	13	52	N/A	14	323

Table 7.10

CASES REGISTERED IN TRIPURA COMMISSION FOR WOMEN IN 2000

DIST.	Total complaints	Bride Killing	Bigamy	Extra Marital Relation	Other domestic violence	Rape	Others	Send to police for proper action	Send to court for proper action	Summon in commission for Counseling and Mitigation
WEST	516	26	33	19	392	9	102	112	16	295
NORTH	61	5	N/A	4	35	3	14	34	10	9
SOUTH	100	4	8	16	45	5	22	57	7	21
DHALAI	23	3	5	2	8	2	3	11	2	6
TOTAL	745	38	46	41	460	19	141	214	35	331

Table 7.11

CASES REGISTERED IN TRIPURA COMMISSION FOR WOMEN IN 1999

DIST.	Total complaints	Bride Killing	Bigamy	Extra Marital Relation	Other domestic violence	Rape	Others	Send to police for proper action	Send to court for proper action	Summon in commission for Counseling and Mitigation
WEST	520	25	38	30	316	11	100	105	31	234
NORTH	69	2	4	9	28	N/A	24	36	N/A	23
SOUTH	102	11	6	8	49	3	28	45	6	30
DHALAI	26	4	2	N/A	12	1	8	16	2	8
TOTAL	717	42	50	47	403	15	160	202	39	495

Table 7.12

CASES REGD. IN TRIPURA COMMISSION FOR WOMEN IN 1998

DIST.	Total complaints	Bride Killing	Bigamy	Extra Marital Relation	Other domestic violence	Rape	Others	Send to police for proper action	Send to court for proper action	Summon in commission for Counseling and Mitigation
WEST	231	14	16	9	180	10	100	88	20	25
NORTH	54	5	6	3	22	6	15	31	1	5
SOUTH	47	5	3	2	24	2	8	51	2	18
DHALAI	27	5	N/A	2	12	N/A	N/A	10	1	5
TOTAL	449	29	25	16	238	18	123	181	24	53

Table 7.13

CASES REGD. IN TRIPURA COMMISSION FOR WOMEN IN 1997

DIST.	Total complaints	Bride Killing	Bigamy	Extra Marital Relation	Other domestic violence	Rape	Others	Send to police for proper action	Send to court for proper action	Summon in commission for Counseling and Mitigation
WEST	236	12	NOT	NOT	NOT	1	223	88	20	25
NORTH	57	4	RE	REC	REC	1	2	31	1	5
SOUTH	87	4	CO	OR	OR	3	4	51	2	18
DHALAI	21	N/A	RD	DE	DE	1	2	10	1	5
TOTAL	401	20	ED	D	D	5	231	181	24	53

Table 7.14
CASES REGD IN TRIPURA COMMISSIOON FOR WOMEN IN 1996

DIST.	Total complaints	Bride Killing	Bigamy	Extra Marital Relation	Other domestic violence	Rape	Others	Send to police for proper action	Send to court for proper action	Summon in commission for Counseling and Mitigation
WEST	238	18	NOT	NOT	NOT	3	217	97	47	22
NORTH	34	2	RE	REC	REC	3	29	20	9	8
SOUTH	56	4	CO	OR	OR	6	46	22	13	5
DHALAI	10	N/A	RD	DE	DE	1	9	7	1	1
TOTAL	338	24	ED	D	D	13	301	148	70	36

Table 7.15

CASES REGISTERED. IN TRIPURA COMMISSIOON FOR WOMEN IN 1995

DIST.	Total complaints	Bride Killing	Bigamy	Extra Marital Relation	Other domestic violence	Rape	Others	Send to police for proper action	Send to court for proper action	Summon in commission for Counseling and Mitigation
WEST	317	12	NOT	NOT	NOT	1	204	210	15	27
NORTH	30	1	RE	REC	REC	N/A	29	6	2	4
SOUTH	49	1	CO	OR	OR	1	47	21	2	4
DHALAI	14	1	RD	DE	DE	1	12	6	1	N/A
TOTAL	410	15	ED	D	D	3	392	243	20	35

Table 7.16
CASES REGISTERED IN TRIPURA COMMISSIOON FOR WOMEN IN 1994

DIST.	Total complaints	Bride Killing	Bigamy	Extra Marital Relation	Other domestic violence	Rape	Others	Send to police for proper action	Send to court for proper action	Summon in commission for Counseling and Mitigation
WEST	136	18	NOT	NOT	NOT	1	117	81	4	25
NORTH	26	3	RE	REC	REC	N/A	23	24	N/A	3
SOUTH	23	4	CO	OR	OR	2	17	14	2	4
DHALAI	N/A	N/A	RD	DE	DE	N/A	N/A	N/A	N/A	N/A
TOTAL	185	25	ED	D	D	3	119	119	6	32

The Tripura State Commission for Women established by the Tripura Government in 1993 started functioning in 1994. It is an apex body for all the women of the state. From the very beginning this body has been functioning from the grass roots level for the protection and empowerment of women in the state. The closest association of TCW with the women of Tripura has been clear from the fact that almost all the tortured and aggrieved women or the family members of the victims approach to the commission with a hope of getting quick remedy and speedy justice.In spite of the fact that the commission is not the law enforcing agency but only a recommending body, which may monitor the functioning of the law-enforcing agency and also not a judicial body, which may pass sentence to justice, yet the women of the state approach this commission for proper implementation of law. Many victims approach the commission as well as the police at the same time with a hope that recommendation of commission may activate the law enforcing machinery.

In this chapter, total crime rate per million persons in different states and union territories and the rate of crime against women in union territories and states as well as distribution of states/UTs by level of total crime rates are adopted from the paper written by C. Mukherjee, P.Rastogi and Krishnaji *[Economics and Political weekly*, Oct. 27th 2001] (Table I, II & III). The tables prepared by them from NCRB data indicate the peculiarity of Tripura. Because in Tripura total crime rate is low, yet the crime rare against women is quite high.

This peculiarity indicates three things:

(1) Reporting of crime against women is too high in Tripura.

(2) The rate of reporting of CAW indicates that the level of consciousness in relation to crime against women is quite high in Tripura. This is probably due to some reasons, which include women's relatively good literacy rate and relatively high educational level, long association of Tripura women with the political movement and the women organizations like their active participation in Panchayat Raj system.

(3) Yet "........... regions with high (low) reported crimes is quite likely to be those with actual high (low) crime rate" (Mukherjee *et al. Ibid.)*. But if we ignore the point of consciousness of Tripura women, then we ignore the positive aspect of women movement in Tripura.

Later on, I presented the data on three types of crime against women in Tripura from Tripura Police data (CID). The tables were prepared districtwise (West, South and North). Tripura has four districts but data on CAW in Dhalai district is not available. The Tripura police data include categories of CAW in their report. These are domestic violence, rape, extremist violence etc. (Table 7.4, 7.5 & 7.6). The police data is too low yet those data also indicate rising reported CAW in three different districts. The peculiarity in police data is that the number of rape cases is more in comparison to the cases of domestic violence.

After that, author presented the detailed data on the cases registered in Tripura Commission for Women, 1994-2002. The number of cases registered in Tripura Commission for Women is quite high in comparision with the cases registered in police station. This is particularly true for the cases of domestic violence.The number of cases registered in the Women Commission has increased from 1994 to 2002. Though the pattern of increase was arbitrary, yet it was increased to a great extent. This is indicative of the fact below:

(1) Faith in Tripura Women Commission is increasing. They gradually become aware of the Women's Commission as an appropriate Commission for redress.

(2) Police largely neglects cases of domestic violences against women. Many of the cases never registered in PS because Tripura Police in general consider domestic violence as 'trivial' or 'private matter'. Women police are not exception. So they refuse to register those cases.

(3) This high number of registered case in TCW also indicates that a large section of women are reluctant to approach to the legal system. They hate and avoid law enforcing machinery for their rude and insensitive behaviour towards the victim and victim's family

members. Some also reluctant to approach to judiciary for the troublesome, lengthy procedure of judiciary. Women victim of domestic violence and rape need speedy justice, quick redress. So they hate to approach this system many a times. They have no money to spend for those purposes also. Sometimes judges are also very insensitive towards women victim though sometime some police personal and judges deal the CAW with great sensitivity. But this is a general impression of Tripura women, which may be applicable to rest of India also.

(4) The large number of registered cases of TCW is indicative of failure of sec 498A to deal with the cases of domestic violence. 498A is the only section that deals with cruelty of husband and in laws at home and also with dowry torture. But real problems of women are not addressed in 498A. Women deserted with children by husbands, rejected/ neglected by in laws find no means to survive. Getting money by filing cases under 125 CrPC is troublesome (Interim relief, final order, realization of money etc. make the total procedure very troublesome for the penniless women suffering with children). Furthermore, jailing of husbands under Sec. 498 ended all their hopes for getting maintenance money form husbands. It is a fact that most of the tortured women never filed any case under Sec. 498A (at least 90%). Here a necessity for a new law to deal with domestic violence becomes urgent cry of every tortured woman. Indira Jai Singh and others from lawyers collective proposed a domestic violence prevention act for this purpose. Government of India also proposed one. But content of it was challenged by different women organization.

(5) The number of cases registered in Women Commission is also indicative of the fact that as Women's Commission has power to look into cases of non-implementation of law, it renders positive impact on police for proper implementation of law. Constant monitoring of Commission delivers results in favour of the women victims.

(6) It is noteworthy that Women's Commission registered all the cases relating to women without any screening. Screening has been done later on and steps are taken as per merit of the case. The cases, which are highly criminal in nature and where compromise or counseling are not possible are being sent to police with a request/ recommendation for proper implementation of law (rape, dowry, death etc) but the cases sent by commission to police are much in number in respect of those cases recorded by police.

(7) The number of cases registered in TCW from west district is very high in comparison to north district. South occupies middle position. The reason for this is that headquarter of TCW is in west. South is more easily connected with west. Communication from north to west is difficult for distance and extremist violence.

Different types of Crime against Women in Tripura as observed from registered cases of TCW

In the last part of author's paper, different types of crime agáinst Tripura women are enlisted :

Those include (1) Domestic violence' (2) Dowry torture and Dowry death, (3) rape, (4) Kidnapping and adduction (immoral trafficking) and (5) Witch hunting.

Author also mentions some special types of crime against women in Tripura related with tribal society and extremism.

Domestic Violence

Some reasons of domestic violence such as bigamy of husband, extramarital relation of husband, alcoholism of husband, child marriage, cases of negligence and torture of old aged women by son/sons and in-laws, parental torture of daughter, violence of women relating the refusal by the brothers to give property, which are registered in the commission with increasing number.

Dowry torture and deaths are rising sharply in Tripura

Due to wide social acceptance of dowry system the dowry laws remain totally ineffective in the state. In spite of wide dowry exchanges no cases were registered so far in Tripura under Dowry Prohibition Act, 498A. It fails to check the crime. Previously 304B (dowry death) was not applied at all in Tripura. Death of bride was generally looked upon as suicide case. Some cases are registered under section 306 but seldom treated under 302 as per post mortem report. Now-a-days police registered more cases of dowry death under section 304B with continuous effort of Women's Commission for proper implementation of law.

Domestic violence and bigamy are rising among the Tripura tribals. Mostly the persons pactising bigamy are government jobholders. But they are trying to avoid the clutch of law in the name of customary law. Neither it is listed properly nor it is codified but the erring and torturous male uses customary law only for their anti women activities.

Surprisingly, the dowry system is spreading among tribals. The tribal women were previously better placed in the society in comparison with Bengali women and some of their marital systems were indicative of female dominance (Jamai Khata). But now these tribals (especially the urban) demand dowry, torture wives for dowry and even kill them. Dowry death among tribals is heart breaking.

Muslims have no religious sanction for dowry system, yet in Tripura, dowry, torture and dowry death among Muslims are also rising in an alarming rate. In the year, 2002, 85 cases of bigamy, refusal by husband to give any maintenance to wife and children, dowry torture and death were registered by the Muslim community to TCW. Forty cases of bigamy, desertion, dowry torture and death were reported from tribal community. Number of total complaints received by the commission in the year 2002 are 657.

Deep rooted feudal mentality of male dominance, unemployment and social insecurity are the root causes of dowry evil. The rising consumerism makes the dowry situation worst day by day in Tripura. Dowry is easy money, which may satisfy unnecessary desire for consumer goods very easily. Women in Tripura in general never get paternal property, though the Bengali Hindus women are legally empowered to get property shares. Yet brothers usually and emotionally exploit them. For this many girls are also willing to get dowry at the time of marriages.

Rape

Rape is the crime, which occupies next in the list of crime against women in Tripura. In the recent past, reported cases of rape of minor girl children have been increased. That is alarming. Tripura people have the painful experience of witnessing the rape incident of a 13 years old girl within Novodaya Vidyalaya complex, South Tripura by the principal of the school. As a consequence of repeated rapes, the helpless girl mothered a child within the hostel complex. TCW helped the minor girl, brought out from the hostel with the new born to file FIR against the offender. The powerful offender creates tremendous pressure from different corners and tries to influence every evidence against him. But the quest of TCW for justice ultimately succeeded. The principal was sentenced to RI life on charge of custodial rape and now languishing in central jail and filed an prayer to high court against the sentence.

Tripura has witnessed the horrifying incident of rape of a minor girl (7 year) and subsequent killing of the raped girl by the rapist. The case is pending before the court of law. In another incident 65-year old person raped a minor girl and poured acid on her private part to destroy the evidence of rape. The rich accused made every effort to influence law-enforcing machinery to avoid punishment. But commission kept its vigil on the aspect of implementation of law. Ultimately the accused found guilty and served 13 years RI on the charge of rape.

Rape of young girls by young boys on the pretexts of false marriages or with false promises of marriages is also rising. The reported number of cases is rising. The conviction rate is slightly increased but still it is less than 5%.

The cruelest part of incidents of rape is that the girls in most of the cases face social rejection. The Navodaya girl was a good student. But some schools refuse to enroll her name. Her parents are reluctant to take her back in home. She is languishing in state home. This is also true for many girls languishing in different homes.

Due to deep-rooted social stigma and social rejection of rape victims, incidents of compromise or dropping out of the cases for some money are very high. This fact straightway fingers out the urgent need of developing a mechanism to give compensation to the rape victims. Apex court gave a clear guideline on the matter of compensation to rape victim. Implementation of it is urgent because only economic independence may fight with social rejection.

There are rising incidents of rape in the tribal area. With the emergence of local armed forces in the hills area, sexual offences are increasing. Sexual offences other than rape like molestation, harassment (eve teasing) are reported to TCW but not to a great extent. Recently a very small number of cases were registered on sexual harassment at workplace. Probably these types of cases have been underreported. An awareness generation among female workers and employees is the foremost step towards implementation of 'Visaka'. The classic example is the non-implementation of Visaka as regards to the lady teachers at the Novodaya Vidyalaya, South Tripura. Many lady teachers of the Novodaya Vidyalaya suffered sexual harassment form that principal who was sentenced for raping the minor student. Later on, if any authority acted as per Visaka judgment, then the rape would never be occurred.

Prior to that incident two lady teachers filed complaint before the authority and the state commission against sexual harassment of the principal. But even with our forwarding, the authority took no steps towards implementation of 'Visaka'. On the contrary they sacked one of the protesting lady teachers. She won her case in CAT and reinstated. Yet the authority continued its harassment towards that lady teacher even after the jailing of the principal. They acted in favour of the person charged and sentenced for rape bur refused to help the lady.

Kidnapping and Abduction

The cases of kidnapping and abduction are of two types:

1) The parents of major and minor girls file cases of kidnapping and abduction when the girls are eloped for marriages.
2) In Tripura, the parents often reject the legal right of their major daughter to marry as per her choice.

Another type of case is trafficking. But immoral trafficking prevention act never applied in our state to deal with any case of trafficking. Police deals with those cases under the specific section of kidnapping and abduction. The cases of trafficking are grossly under reported. But recently it is indicated that there exists trafficking of minor child within state for prostitution. Inter state trafficking and cross border trafficking also being taken place. Commission started to investigate the depth and extent of the problem.

Some other special types of Cases of Crime Against WOMEN: Witch Hunting

Belief in witchcraft is age old among the tribals and it is a deep-rooted belief.

But recently a trend was developed among some of the offenders within tribal community to kill women on the pretext of witch haunting to satisfy their self-interest. Even sometime some groups of extremist branded some outspoken progressive ladies who dare to fight their ideology as witch and killed them. Lakshmi Dev Burma of Tairaj Bari was victim of such kind of offence. Our state may need special law to stop witch hunting.

Extremist Violence on Women

Extremist killed armed tribal and nontribal women when they attack any village. That is a known fact of Tripura. In recent past Tripura has witnessed the painful incident of abduction of minor girl by extremist for ransom. I am sure that this phenomenon has not presented anywhere in India where extremist exists. Killing of exceptional and progressive tribal ladies for opposing extremist ideology is another painful crime witnessed by people in Tripura.

As author mentions earlier, rape was a rare phenomenon in tribal society. But in recent past the local armed tribal boys gang raped non tribal and tribal girls (Raiabari in Taidu). That is also a very painful experience. Incidents of rape are on the rise in tribal areas with the emergence of local armed people associated with extremist.

Incincidence of Para-military Violence on Tribal Women

In a conflict situation, long presence of paramilitary or military forces in a region often caused enormous distress to the local women. This must be very distressing situation for all the women. One can naturally assume. But in Tripura cases of rape, molestation or any other harassment by security forces are seldom reported by anyone.

Commission received 3-4 cases (or took sue moto notice of it from newspaper report) of such kind within 9 years of its function. Commission investigates all the cases and recommends for taking up step against the offenders if they are found guilty by the Commission. But such less number of cases indicate either such types of cases are rare in Tripura due to strict vigilance of Government on functionary of security forces or it may be due to underreporting (especially by the media). Whatever it may be, this type of incident is less in Tripura other than extremist prone areas of the country as indicated by the reported cases.

Conclusion

Inspite of extremism, crime rate is really low in Tripura. But why reported CAW is very high in Tripura? Here are some comments on it.

1) The reporting of CAW in Tripura is very high. This is a

positive outcome not a negative one. The reporting itself proved the people of Tripura started their fight against CAW with the help of government machinery and judiciary system.

2) Tendency of police to register the cases as CAW probably increased to some extent in the recent past.

3) We can see from our discussion that it is not a fact that the crime against women outside is very large in Tripura (excluding some special type of crime) but domestic violence, dowry torture and death are increasing rapidly. It is attributed to the deep-rooted male dominant patriarchal attitude that ruled the mind of the major section of the people of Tripura till today. Still now majority of the Tripura people reject the domestic violence as violence at all. Like the parents feel beating up of child as their right, most of the Tripura male and female (even female police) think torture by husbands, in laws, parents have nothing to do with law. Desertion of wife with dependent kids seldom attracts sympathy from public rather they become sympathetic to the male.

4) Though Tripura women have long history of association with political movements, they are generally launched to strengthen the political parties and to meet political demands. But women seldom emerged as a pressure group to fight the CAW within and outside family.

   Many NGOs are working in the state. But they also seldom acted as a pressure group to prevent violence against women. But these tendencies are now changing. If the women organizations and NGOs start functioning as pressure groups then CAW especially domestic violence will surely be reduced.

5) Tripura has gone through a conflict stage. Tripura is an isolated state from the rest of India. The movement of people is restricted by the insecurity due to extremism. The inevitable outcome of this situation is a stagnant society. Patriarchy is dominant here and on the other side women of Tripura have relatively high literacy rate,

education and work participation. So they are raising their voice against discrimination and violence against women within family.

Conflict within family increases violence against women. I apprehend that in near future not only the recorded crime but also the actual crime against women may increase. With increased participation of women outside may increase violence against women in outside world also. But after that bitter initial rise we will surely progress towards a gender just family and society.

8

Violence against Women in Tripura

A Situational Analysis

—Paramita

There can hardly be any disagreement over the fact that, the world in which we live in, is steeped in violence and no one can really escape the consequences. Violence that pervades every region of this world, every moment of our lives, scenes of violence, fictitious and real, that we see in the visual media, the stories that we read in print, all combine to shape the social psyche and attitude. Today, violence is being increasingly looked upon as an instrument to realize desired objects, to assert authority and dominance, to acquire and establish power by governments and forces opposed to it, alike. The same story is repeated with respect to individuals both when acting alone or in groups. Given this backdrop it hardly surprises anybody that "violence committed against women in one form or the other, is a universal phenomenon prevalent in every region and society, irrespective of the social or economic class to which the women belong". *(Women & Men in India,* 2000). While men also are victims of violence, violence against women is characterized by its high prevalence within the family, its acceptance by society and its serious long-term effect on women's health and well-being. (*Outlook*, 2002).

The increasing concern about violence against women, particularly in developing countries arises from the concern for women empowerment. Violence against women has long been recognized as a major obstacle in the process of women empowerment. It is now widely accepted that development in the true sense cannot materialize without empowering women. Viewed in this larger context of development, violence against women has far reaching consequences. Violence against women is a serious obstacle to development, peace and equality (*Yojana*, 2001). Apart from causing physiological and psychological damages to the victim, violence inflicts enormous cost to the society in terms of drain on the economically productive work force and undue burden on the health system. Despite the seriousness of the problem in terms of violation of human rights and public health consequences, there is a dearth of knowledge on the extent and nature of violence against women for various reasons. Of them methodological difficulties in studying the problem are the important ones. (Bhuiya, Sharmin and Hanifi 2003)

Violence against girls and women often starts even before they are born and can continue throughout their lives into old ages (Watts, *et. al.* 2003). In Indian society there is strong preference for male child and female foeticide (selective abortion of female foetus) is reported to be not very uncommon (Sudha and Rajan,1999). In some parts of the country female infanticide is an age-old practice. People in Tripura as well as in North East are believed to be much more tolerant towards the girl-child. Yet instances of violence against women who have failed to give birth to male children are quite common. Beginning with the nutritional deprivation from the early childhood, woman throughout her entire life stage confronts a violent world. Most of them compromise, accept and even rationalize all ill treatments (Jaisingh, 1995; Hegde, 1996; Prasad, 1999). The culture of silence and acceptance combined with the sense of shame with which a girl-child is brought up act a curtain and in most cases incidences of violence are not reported.

Two important areas of investigation are the extent of violence against women and the nature of impact of violence on the women, the family and the society. One major difficulty in studying different aspects of violence against women is unavailability of data. Generation of primary data is also difficult as women are in general reluctant to talk about their experiences of violence within and outside home. Moreover, data collection to have an idea about the scale and magnitude of the situation of violence against women becomes difficulty in the absence of consensus on what constitutes violence. The Declaration on the Elimination of Violence against Women (1993) defines violence against women as "any act of gender-based violence that results in or is likely to result in physical, sexual or mental harm or suffering to women, including threats of such acts, coercion or arbitrary deprivation of liberty, whether occurring in public or in private life".

This encompasses, inter alia, "physical, sexual and psychological violence occurring in the family and in the general community, including battering, sexual abuse of children, dowry-related violence, female genital mutilation and other traditional practices harmful to women, non-spousal violence related to exploitation, sexual harassment and intimidation at work, in educational institutions and elsewhere, trafficking in women, forced prostitution and violence perpetrated or condoned by the state." However, the definition of violence is largely determined by the individual's perception of different acts based on social cultural norms. There may be women who do not report their experiences of domestic violence because they do not view them violence (NFHS-II).

The impact study requires detailed data, for example on the number of lost days of work due to violence, expenditure on treatment of physical injury caused by violence, apart from assessing the cost of psychological damages. World Bank estimates that violence against women is as great a cause of death and incapacity among women of reproductive age as cancer, and a greater cause of ill health than traffic accidents and malaria combined. (World Development Report, 1993).

The phenomenon of violence against women may be universal but policies for addressing the issue and preventive measures must be culture specific. Hence, the need for collecting and interpreting data on violence against women in different regions for designing preventive interventions cannot be over emphasized. The present paper thus has a limited objective and seeks to present the situation in Tripura in this regard.

The paper is divided into four sections. Section one introduces the topic and highlights the importance of undertaking studies and research on different aspects of violence against women. Attitude of women in Tripura towards violence against them is analyzed in section two. Section three provides an idea about the extent of violence in the state on the basis of newspaper reports. Interpretations of the findings are given in section four.

II

The instances of violence against women in any society, as reported in crime statistics, in newspapers, in police records and the like, are most likely to underestimate the extent of prevalence of violence. For each instance reported, there are many others, which go unreported. Usually, violence is reported only in extreme situation when there is a death or a possibility of death. Domestic violence against women, especially beating wives by husbands are seldom complained about. Thus it is hardly possible to quantify the extent of violence against women in terms of concrete figures. However, the cases reported in newspapers provide important insights into the prevailing social context in which violence takes place against women.

Violence against women may be broadly grouped as violence within and outside household. Usually violence within home, i.e. domestic violence is considered synonymous to wife-beating and related abuses. But it would be more appropriate to include violence against girl-child also in this category. In poor households children are often looked upon as producer goods and particularly the pre-teens or teenage girls are found working outside home e.g. collection of fire wood, fetching water, working as domestic helps. All these make her vulnerable to the risk of violence.When the mother is physically abused in the household; the children are likely to grow up accepting the observed behavior as a norm. The girl-child is likely to be neglected and deprived of nutrition, healthcare and education. She will in all probability grow up accepting the patriarchal dictate. The boy, on the other hand will grow up into man with the belief that wife-beating is an acceptable way of disciplining the woman and more likely to perpetuate wife abuse as an adult (Heise 1998).

Violence against women within the household by the husband and the family members occurs due to various reasons like property disputes, inability to give birth to male child, infertility, failure of the natal family to provide money, jewelry and other items during marriage etc. An attempt in the National Family Health Survey II was made to assess women's attitude towards wife beating. All the married women in age group of 15-49 years were asked whether they think the husband is justified in beating his wife for specific reasons like if he suspects her of being unfaithful, if her natal family did not give expected amount of dowry, if she shows disrespect for her in-laws, if she goes out without his permission, if she neglects house or children or if she does not cook properly. Acceptance of at least one of these specific reasons as justified ground for wife-beating reveals the attitude of women towards violence.

The data show that acceptance of unequal power relations between husbands and wives is much lower in Tripura than in India as a whole, and is the lowest among the northeastern states. Only 37.5 per cent respondents in Tripura thought that husbands are justified to beat the wife at least on one of the above-mentioned grounds. The corresponding figure for India as a whole is 56 per cent. In

Table 8.1

WOMEN'S ATTITUDE TOWARDS WIFE-BEATING

Percentage who agree with specific reasons:

	Percentage who agree with at least one reason	Husband suspects wife is unfaithful	Natal family does not give expected money or other items	Wife shows dierespect for in-laws	Wife goes out without telling	Wife neglects house	Wife does not cook food children husband properly
Mizoram	83.6	33.4	5.4	52.2	42.8	68.2	7.1
Nagaland	96.9	92.7	16.7	79.6	60.3	84.9	32.9
Tripura	37.5	16.8	5.8	21.8	19.1	22.2	14.9
Arunachal Pradesh	51.3	10.2	4.8	37.3	30.3	44.5	26.2
Manipur	91.3	34.1	3.5	76.5	69.1	83.2	15.3
Meghalaya	86.1	44.2	19.6	47.8	63.8	78.0	36.6

Source : National Family Health Survey 2, 1998-1999

Tripura, acceptance declines sharply with education. In other northeastern states, however, acceptance does not vary consistently with education. In Manipur it does not vary at all with education. Acceptance also declines sharply with household per standard of living. Only 21 per cent of women from households with high standard of living agreed to at least one reason for which they thought the husband is justified in wife beating. This was 47 per cent for women belonging to household with low standard of living.

According to the National Family Health Survey prevalence of domestic violence in Tripura is higher in rural areas than in urban areas. In Tripura, most of the women who reported beatings are of their husbands who physically mistreated them. Women rarely report beatings by in-laws. Prevalence of violence is strongly and negatively associated with level of education and household standard of living in Tripura. In other northeastern states, however this does not hold uniformly true.

III

Incidences of violence committed against women are not limited only to wife beating by the husband and relatives. This also includes rape, molestation, dowry related abuse often leading to death or suicide, kidnapping, abduction, immoral trafficking of girls etc. A quick overview may be obtained regarding prevalence of various crimes against women from the local newspaper reports.

Though the time of the day may be an important factor for the incidence of violence to take place, it can safely be assumed that there is no seasonal pattern in the occurrences of violence against women. Hence the month of July 2003 was selected and the daily editions of a widely circulated local vernacular newspaper in Bengali were thoroughly scrutinized. It is observed that almost everyday the newspaper carried reports on incidences of violence against women. In all forty cases were reported in these thirty-one days. There were also reports on the progress of investigations and conviction in cases of violence that took place earlier.

Sometimes incidences in other parts of the country were also reported. The total number of incidences includes all cases, which took place in different parts of Tripura only, but have not necessarily taken place in the month of July itself. The follow up reports of various incidents are excluded from this total number. The following table no.2 shows the number of different crimes which have been reported during the reference period.

Out of nine murders reported five were dowry-related and out of eleven cases of physical assaults, wife-beatings etc., five took place due to dowry. One disturbing fact is the prevalence of dowry related offences in tribal families also. It shows how the practices of dominant community influence the social behaviour patterns of other groups.

Table 8.2
TYPES OF VIOLENCE AND NUMBERS

(As reported during July 20003)

Types	No. of Incidence
Murder	9
Rape	8
Physical assault	11
Suicide	6
Molestation	3
others	4
Total	41

Source: Compiled from newspaper reports.

Other reasons for physical assaults on women include failure to give birth to a son, suspicion of being a witch, disputes on property matters etc. In one instance the panchayat members assaulted and forcibly evicted a widow and her daughters from her home after she refused to handover her land for construction of a proposed bus-stand. Out of six, four suicides were reported due to dowry related torture .In other two cases torture by in-laws cited as the cause of suicide though no reason of torture was specified in the reports. Conviction of persons involved in a racket procuring and selling girls for prostitution in other states is also reported. Eight cases of rapes are reported in the reference period. Three of the victims were minor girls and two were murdered after being raped. The issue of violence against women acquires another dimension when we come to the northeastern part of our country. In situation of armed conflict, extremism etc the threat of violence against women increases manifold. It has been observed that women are at the receiving end and are the worst sufferers as they become victims of both terrorist groups and security personnel deployed for combating terrorism and extremism. Cases of rapes and torture by terrorist groups are not usually reported due to fear. One report, however, records indecent behaviour with women by security personnel.

Another issue which has not received much attention until recently is the increasing threat of violence against elderly persons particularly elderly women. With the increase of life expectancy, number of elderly people is increasing day by day. Elderly women are vulnerable to violence both within and outside home. In areas with extremist problems the situation becomes grave. Often they are left behind when family members run for cover during extremist attacks, and they bear the brunt of their ire. Families displaced due to extremist problems cannot take care of their elderly family members in the face of economic hardships. Conditions of elderly women in relief camps are pitiable. Incidences of elderly abuse within the family are rarely reported. But cases of violence against elderly women, who are widowed and are living alone, often make way to the newspapers. Burning, beating and rape of elderly women have been reported in recent times. Though no such case was reported during the reference period, it should not imply that such types of incidences do not occur.

IV

All these events of rapes, murders, molestation, illegal trafficking of girls, physical assault of women by husbands and families underscore the increasing influence of lust and greed in our society. Incidences of rape and molestation of minor girls studying in schools are being frequently reported. In many cases it is one of the teachers, who is in the criminal act. The Navodaya Vidyalaya incident is a case in point. In one of the rare occasions the accused principal of the school was sentenced to life imprisonment. The role of Tripura State Commission for Women was laudable in this case. When the teacher who is supposed to act as protector himself turns out to be a perpetrator, one must look into where the rot has set in. Another disturbing aspect is the involvement of young teenage boys in cases of rapes and molestations. The impact of overexposure to sex and violence through a globalized television media is too obvious to be overlooked and ignored. In a globalized economic environment it is difficult to escape the invasion of the media by images of women depicted in a manner which does not conform to our cultural ethos. The erotic and vulgar display of woman's body in product advertisements and music videos provokes young minds into forbidden ventures. The only way to combat this is proper education and awareness among young girls and boys.

Dowry deaths and dowry related torture of women is an issue, which continues to make the headlines almost everyday. The customary practice of giving money and after gifts as dowry during marriage by the natal family of the bride to the bridegroom's family has existed in Bengali Hindu society since long. Giving one's own daughter material gifts of jewelry, money, land etc. in marriage was considered a holy deed- a way to earn 'Punya'.

In traditional tribal society, however, there existed 'bride-price' wherein the prospective bridegroom had to pay for marrying a girl. Sometimes we had to prove his worth by staying and working in the house of his prospective bride. But now a days this is no longer the case. Instances of demand for dowry and torture of bride for dowry in tribal families are also coming to the fore.

In a society where daughters' shares in the parental property are not easily obtained and inheritance laws are difficult to enforce, the customs of dowry ensure that the daughters at least get something. The custom of dowry can also be looked upon as a security provision for the girl by her father. On the part of the bridegroom's family, dowry is a compensation offered by bride's family to the bridegroom as he takes up her lifelong responsibility. As girls are not educated enough and lack in the human capital necessary to earn their livelihood, they are usually dependent upon the husbands. In poor families, however, the uneducated women have always been working and earning for the families. But dowry exists even when the girl is educated enough, employed and earning. In a large number of cases the working bride, in addition to bringing dowry is expected to give up the right over her own earnings by depositing the same to the husband or mother-in-law perhaps as compensations for her absence from home for outside work and presumed neglect of household duties.

Fascination for a highly consumerist lifestyle propagated by the media often lures people into using the easy option to demand dowry to procure desired objects of material comfort. In our society where family is considered more important than the individual, it is no wonder that women accept all these undue demands and tolerate tortures silently for the sake of family and children. Once married, the paternal family is most unwilling to support her, if she wants to leave her husband's place. Often they pressurize her to adjust to her husband and his family. In extreme cases she is murdered or is forced to commit suicide. Even when the woman is economically self dependent, she finds it difficult to escape from the violence meted out to her due to the unavailability of support mechanism. It is in this sphere that NGO and Tripura State Commission for Women can step in.

Policies for preventive interventions cannot be based on legal provisions alone. As legal process is long drawn and expensive, a large number of women do not access to it. Therefore, in addition to legal provisions, the policies should incorporate building of community based resistance groups for checking violence against women. In the long run social vigilance and awareness are going to be the most crucial factors in the prevention of violence against women.

References

Bhuiya, Abbas, Tamanna, Sharmin and S.M.A. Hanifi, 2003: Nature of Domestic Violence Against Women in a Rural Area of Bangladesh: Implication for preventive intervensions. Journal of Health Population, Nutrition March 2003, 21 (1): 48 - 54

Hegde, Radha S. 1996: Narratives of Silence: Rethinking gender, agency and power from the communication experiences of battered women in South India: Communication Studies 47: 303-317.

Heise, L. 1998 Violence Against Women: An Integrated Ecological Framework: Violence Against Women: 1998 4: 262-90.

Jaisingh, I. 1995: Violence Against Women: The Indian Perspective, in J.Peters & A.Wolper (eds.), Women's Rights, Human Rights. New York: Routledge.

Prasad, Shally 1999: Medicolegal response to violence against women in India, Violence Against Women 5(5): 478-506.

Sudha, S. and Rajan, S.I. 1993: Female demographic disadvantage in India 1981-1991: Sex selective abortion and female infanticide. Development and Change, Special Issue on Gendered Poverty and Well-being 1995 30: 585-618.

Watts, C. and Zimmerman, C.2002: Violence Against Women, global scope and magnitude. The Lancet April 6, 2002, 359 (9313): 1232-1237.

Men and Women in India 2000, Central Statistical Organisations.

National Family Health Survey, India, North- Eastern States 1998-99, International Institute for Population Sciences.

World Bank. World Development Report 1993: Investing in Health. New York: Oxford University Press 1993.

❑❑❑

Index

●●●